Chinese Signs

Highlighting stylistic and rhetorical characteristics, this fully illustrated book explores the written form of Mandarin Chinese in a range of everyday settings. Taking examples from Chinese public writing across a variety of textual genres, such as signs, banners and advertisements, it prepares students for navigating 'real world' Chinese, not only in terms of its linguistic and stylistic characteristics, but also its social and cultural context. Drawing over 500 pictorial examples from the linguistic landscape, it explores the signs from a variety of perspectives, for example by highlighting elements of classical Chinese that are still used in the modern language, showing the most popular rhetorical patterns used in Chinese, and presenting the interactions between both Standard Mandarin and dialect, and Chinese and other languages. Detailed annotations are provided for all signs, in both Chinese and English, to accommodate readers of all proficiency levels in Chinese.

Zheng-sheng Zhang is Professor at the Department of Linguistics and Asian/Middle Eastern Languages, San Diego State University. Recent publications include *Dimensions of Variation in Written Chinese* (2017) and *Introduction to Chinese Natural Language Processing* (co-authored, 2009).

Chinese Signs

An Introduction to China's Linguistic Landscape

ZHENG-SHENG ZHANG

San Diego State University

CAMBRIDGE
UNIVERSITY PRESS

Shaftesbury Road, Cambridge CB2 8EA, United Kingdom

One Liberty Plaza, 20th Floor, New York, NY 10006, USA

477 Williamstown Road, Port Melbourne, VIC 3207, Australia

314–321, 3rd Floor, Plot 3, Splendor Forum, Jasola District Centre, New Delhi – 110025, India

103 Penang Road, #05-06/07, Visioncrest Commercial, Singapore 238467

Cambridge University Press is part of Cambridge University Press & Assessment, a department of the University of Cambridge.

We share the University's mission to contribute to society through the pursuit of education, learning and research at the highest international levels of excellence.

www.cambridge.org

Information on this title: www.cambridge.org/9781108839068

DOI: 10.1017/9781108979603

First published 2024

A catalogue record for this publication is available from the British Library

Library of Congress Cataloging-in-Publication Data
Names: Zhang, Zheng-sheng, author.
Title: Chinese signs : an introduction to China's linguistic landscape / Zheng-sheng Zhang, San Diego State University.
Description: Cambridge ; New York, NY : Cambridge University Press, 2024. | Includes bibliographical references and index.
Identifiers: LCCN 2023033777 (print) | LCCN 2023033778 (ebook) | ISBN 9781108839068 (hardback) | ISBN 9781108969697 (paperback) | ISBN 9781108979603 (epub)
Subjects: LCSH: Chinese language–Writing. | Chinese language–Study and teaching–English speakers. | Mandarin dialects–Study and teaching–English speakers. | Signs and signboards–China.
Classification: LCC PL1171 .Z45826 2024 (print) | LCC PL1171 (ebook) | DDC 495.11/1–dc23/eng/20231103
LC record available at https://lccn.loc.gov/2023033777
LC ebook record available at https://lccn.loc.gov/2023033778

ISBN 978-1-108-83906-8 Hardback
ISBN 978-1-108-96969-7 Paperback

CONTENTS

Contents

Contents

ACKNOWLEDGMENTS

The gemination of the idea for a collection of authentic materials for teaching Chinese goes back at least three decades. In the early 1990s, I was part of a group in Southern California thinking about developing alternative teaching materials. One of the ideas was a set of authentic materials we jokingly referred to as 百宝箱 'treasure box.' The current book may not have lived up to what was envisioned, but I wish to thank my like-minded colleagues for sharing the desire for authentic materials.

I wish to thank my departmental colleagues Professors Eniko Csomay and Rob Malouf, who first inspired me to investigate stylistic variation using corpora.

Thanks go my San Diego State University students of my 2011 experimental course entitled 'Variety of Authentic Written Chinese,' where I first implemented my research on style in Chinese. Thanks also go to the cadets in a similar class at the US Air Force Academy, where I taught from 2017 to 2019.

Lastly, I am grateful to my wife Xi and daughter Natalie for their steadfast support, and for tolerating my long absence when I went away first to the US Air Force Academy and then to Kyrgyzstan as a Fulbright scholar. They also provided the initial impetus for a sign-collecting trip to Shanghai in the winter of 2019, when the majority of the pictures were taken.

Part I
General Characteristics

1   Why Signs?

The first question a reader may ask is: Why devote a whole book to Chinese signs? At least three reasons can perhaps be given:

1. Signs represent an important part of the Chinese linguistic landscape.
2. The ability to read signs is essential for surviving and thriving in the Chinese world.
3. Signs make for good materials for learning Chinese.

Signs as Part of the Linguistic Landscape

Signs are seen anywhere in the world. But they seem more numerous in China, particularly if we consider the civic and political banners that are seen everywhere. With their omnipresence and easy access, signs provide an easy window into the world of Chinese language and society.

The contents of signs can reflect important social issues of the day, such as food safety, wastefulness, and environmental degradation. A glance at the current political banners will give you an inkling of what is going on in the country. There must be a reason why 文明 "civilization" is such a buzzword in signs. Signs are also barometers of changing times. The sightings of many foreign businesses such as KFC, Starbucks, Walmart, McDonalds, and Carrefour are concrete signs (pun intended) of the Reform and Opening up that started over four decades ago, while the recent plan to eliminate English translations in traffic signs once again reflects China's vacillating attitude toward foreign influences.

The choices regarding language and form in signs also reflect language attitudes, and the cultural associations of these choices. What is official may not always be what is chosen. In Hong Kong, the author first saw Cantonese writing using the letter "D" in lieu of the Cantonese 啲 or the standard 点 to express the meaning "a bit" (Apart from the openness towards mixing scripts, "D" really sounds closer to the Cantonese word than 点 and is easier to type than 啲). Many overseas scholars originally from the mainland have chosen to write in traditional characters, which cannot be solely attributed to conforming to local preference.

The existing literature on the Chinese linguistic landscape (for example Guo and Li 2017; Shang 2020; Wang 2013) mostly focuses on ethnolinguistic and socio-political issues such as ethnic identity, semiotic functions, multilingualism, language choice, and language policy, but devotes less attention to the formal features of signs themselves, including their very distinct stylistic and rhetorical characteristics. Also lacking is the use of signs for the learning of Chinese. To complement existing work, this book aims to focus on the following aspects of signs:

> The formal and written style
> Classical Chinese elements
> Special lexical and grammatical features
> Common rhetorical devices
> Dialectal and foreign words and how they are written
> Character styles and text orientation

The difference between the written and the spoken style in Chinese is so drastic that it is characterized as a "gulf" by Li and Thompson (1982). Signs are good examples of the written style, with its distinct lexical and syntactic characteristics. They are replete with classical Chinese elements. Even the sign for entrance 入口 contains the classical word 入. Signs can flaunt grammatical rules, in having more flexible syntactic function and word order. They often contain background-dependent "out of vocabulary" items such as aliases and abbreviations. Fleeting ad hoc abbreviations headed by numbers such as 五讲四美 are particularly opaque.

Signs accentuate rhetorical preferences deeply ingrained in the culture, such as the fondness for punning and the predilection for parallelism and symmetry. These rhetorical preferences are quite pervasive and are seen even in mundane contexts such as the warnings over urinals 贴近方便, 靠近文明 (see Chapter 17).

The cultural and regional diversity of China is inevitably reflected in signs, which can incorporate dialectal elements, especially from the more prominent Cantonese, Min, and Shanghai dialects.

More and more foreign elements are spotted on the Chinese linguistic landscape. The author experienced a shock when visiting a shopping mall in the coastal city of Ningbo a few years ago. In the whole shopping mall, not a single store had its name in Chinese characters, even though most of the stores were not foreign. Foreign-sounding names of businesses are also quite common.

Diversity is also seen in the choice of character style and text orientation. In mainland China, traditional characters are still occasionally used instead of simplified characters. It is not uncommon to see them on business cards, which convey the appearance of learnedness. Store signs sometimes also choose traditional characters to evoke a sense of nostalgia and of course tradition. Text orientation also varies, especially in places like Taiwan, where traditional vertical and right to left lines co-exist with the modern left-to-right orientation.

The Ability to Read Signs Is a Practical Necessity

Signs serve real-world functions; and ability to decipher them is essential in navigating the Chinese world. But there has been an apparent paradox regarding the use of signs for language teaching: the ability to read public signs is unquestionably necessary for survival; at the same time, there is a glaring gap in the typical language curriculum: students are hardly exposed to signs at all, even at the advanced levels of studies. Books on reading Chinese signs have been few (Kubler 1993 is a notable exception).

The general neglect may be attributed to the blind spots that native curriculum developers likely suffer from. Indeed, it took a non-native scholar to point out the paradox: the most basic survival skill is not taught. The avoidance of signs may also be due to the belief that they are too difficult for learners. Signs typically employ classical Chinese lexical and grammatical features. The difficulty in reading signs may be due to another kind of blind spot, the aforementioned "out of vocabulary" items (items typically not found in dictionaries) such as aliases of place names, somewhat ad hoc abbreviations whose interpretation heavily depends on knowledge of current affairs.

Signs Make Good Learning Materials

Even though they have not received sufficient attention in the standard curriculum, using signs as teaching material makes good pedagogical sense.

Signs are public, easily accessible, and thus provide free resources for learning about China and the Chinese language. Signs are authentic. They are not written by textbook writers, nor simplified in any way. They are more authentic than typical pedagogical materials in another way. To attract attention, many signs are rendered in artistically enhanced (cursive, outlined, or distorted) fonts, which may be harder to read than text in typical textbooks.

As the style of written Chinese is accentuated on signs, studying signs can heighten the sensitivity to stylistic difference between writing and speech. As they are replete with classical Chinese elements, signs can also serve as a more motivated and gentler introduction to classical Chinese, motivated by their practicality and made easier by the smaller dosage. In learning to read signs, students can acquire the most frequently used classical Chinese elements in modern contexts.

The practical nature of signs provides intrinsic motivation for learning them. Signs may be less daunting psychologically to learners, as they are typically short, often in fragment or phrasal form. They are also easier to remember as they are loaded with contextual information. Finally, bilingual signs and translation mistakes in them can accentuate the differences between the two languages.

General Learning Objectives

When used as teaching material, the general learning objectives include:

1. Increasing awareness of the style of public writing
2. Acquiring common classical Chinese elements
3. Gaining familiarity with 'out of vocabulary' items such as aliases and abbreviations
4. To gaining familiarity with rhetorical devices such as punning and parallelism
5. Exposure to the great diversity in China's linguistic landscape
6. Gaining familiarity with how dialect and foreign words are written in China.

Intended Audience

With its wealth of authentic signs, the book can be used in a dedicated course on Chinese signage and for students and researchers interested in linguistic landscapes. The volume can also be used as a supplemental resource book for a course at any level in a Chinese curriculum. As the signs can differ in length and complexity, they can be selectively used with learners with a wide range of backgrounds and proficiency in Chinese. As the signs will be thoroughly annotated and explained in detail, they should be comprehensible to anyone, including travelers and tourists going to China. The practical aspect of this book should make it attractive to any potential student, who wants to be able to function in the real world of Chinese.

Signs Included in This Volume

In this volume, the definition of public signage is interpreted in the broadest sense. Road signs, traffic signs, warning signs, ads, banners, couplets, and advertising billboards have all been sampled. In terms of length, they range from a few characters to multiple lines.

For many years now, the author has been collecting images of signs from personal trips to various locations in China, including Beijing, Shanghai, Xiamen, Quanzhou, Yunnan, Xi'an and Xinjiang. During the winter break of 2019–2020, the author undertook another signs-collecting expedition to China and took more than 1,000 photos of various signs. Noteworthy examples are selected for this book. Greater attention is given to signs that show special cultural, linguistic, and stylistic characteristics.

Signs from Taiwan and Hong Kong are also included, collected from past trips. This provides an interesting counterpoint to mainland signs, with lexical and orthographical differences.

Selected signs from the Chinese diaspora are also included. They are particularly important for the study of linguistic landscape, as they are relevant to issues such as linguistic choice, multilingualism, immigration history, ethnic identity, and political allegiance. Bilingual or multi-lingual diaspora signs also need to resolve the problem of how to cope with other languages. Only the signs that show differences particular to diaspora contexts are featured in Chapter 19. Some diaspora signs can also be found in other chapters. The diaspora signs in this volume are mostly from English-speaking regions. The author also collected some signs in Dungan (a Northwest Chinese dialect) written in the Cyrillic alphabet from his 2021–2022 Fulbright year in Kyrgyzstan.

It needs to be noted that the signs included in this volume are by no means exhaustive. They are limited by the author's personal experience and circumstances. An obvious lacuna is signs on sports and sports venues.

Presentation Format

The signs are all from original photos taken by the author, albeit cropped to save space and eliminate distracting elements. Annotations include the following information:

Chinese text will be typed out. Simplified characters and left-to-right and horizontal orientation will be uniformly used, even when the original signs are in traditional format and characters. This provides an opportunity for comparison.

Pronunciation is indicated in pinyin. The usual convention regarding the marking of tone changes has been adopted. Tone changes of third-tone syllables are not marked; the tone change rule should be applied when read. The changed tone of 不 and 一 are given. Neutral tones are marked.

Meaning gloss. Meaning glosses are separated from pinyin by a vertical bar "|". Unlike typical vocabulary lists, which only gloss whole words, the glossing of meaning in this book is done in three different ways, depending on which is more appropriate for the item in question:

1. When the meaning of the whole word is predictable from the meanings of its parts, only meanings of the component characters will be given. Glossing the component characters can make the meaning of compound words more transparent and more relatable to other words sharing the same components. For example, 轻食 "light meal" will be glossed as 轻 "light" and 食 "food", which can be related to and contrasted with compounds such as 熟食 "cooked food". To save space and avoid duplication, glosses for the whole words will also be omitted, when the signs are bilingual with good English translations. Character-by-character gloss may be done selectively.

2. Character-by-character gloss sometimes is not possible with words whose meanings do not seem derivable from the meanings of their components in a transparent manner. An example is 经济 "economy", the meanings of whose components are quite opaque (the classical etymological explanation 经世济民 notwithstanding.) Then only the whole compound word is glossed.

3. Sometimes, the meanings of the whole words are relatable to the meanings of their component morphemes, but there is enough difference between the two. In such cases, both meanings of the component characters and those of the whole words are given. The component characters are glossed because the meanings of the component characters obviously contribute to the meaning of the whole words. The whole words are glossed too because their meanings are not quite the same as the sum of the meaning of the component characters. For example, in addition to glossing 美食 as "gourmet food", its components are individually glossed as beautiful (美) and food (食). The meaning of the whole compound word is given for accuracy, while the meanings of the components are given to help with understanding and retention. It may happen that even in the same sign, some words are translated component by component, while others are translated by the whole word. To distinguish between glosses on component morphemes and those on whole words, the latter will be enclosed in parentheses.

Also provided are notes about other noteworthy characteristics, including:

> grammatical particularities
> classical elements
> rhetorical devices used
> contextual and background information
> style and stylistic alternatives

Learning Outcomes

To accentuate the main foci, some learning outcomes are given at the end of each chapter before the suggested learning activities.

Suggested Learning Activities

Some learning activities will be suggested at the end of each chapter. They include the following:

> Using suggested key terms, search online for similar signs as presented in the chapter.
> Using alternative character style to search for signs of the same kind from other regions.

Type out the text of the found signs.

Translate signs, to check comprehension and note the differences between languages.

Identify classical Chinese elements, aliases, and abbreviations in found signs.

Paraphrase written style in spoken style.

Identify foreign and dialectal elements.

Identify puns, parallelism, and other rhetorical devices.

Analyze translation strategies in bilingual signs.

Analyze mistakes in translation and correct them.

Ordering from the restaurant menus provided.

Use signs in a narrative on a related topic (e.g. a train journey.)

Design a sign by following models, with stylistically appropriate words.

Using a corpus (bcc.blcu.edu.cn/) to check the frequency and time of certain terms.

Using (part of) a line from a couplet, search online for the matching line.

Organization of the Book

The twenty-one chapters of the volume are divided into three parts.

The first part (Chapters 1–4) is a general introduction to the main linguistic, rhetorical, and formal characteristics of Chinese signs.

The second part (Chapters 5–15) presents essential and practical signs.

The third part (Chapters 16–20) will cover more advanced signs, such as ads, civic and political banners, and signs with dialectal and foreign elements. Chapter 19 is devoted to the Chinese diaspora; Chapter 20 covers foreign elements.

There is a supplemental chapter (Chapter 21) on translation mistakes in bilingual signs, which will be categorized and analyzed.

An alphabetically sorted index and an index of signs with Chinese and English keywords.

Stylistic Traits

This chapter presents select signs that show several common stylistic traits of written Chinese. These include classical Chinese elements, mixed lexical compounds with both classical and non-classical components, and classical Chinese grammatical features. There are also many 'out of vocabulary' items not usually found in dictionaries. They include aliases for place names and the numerous ad hoc and fleeting abbreviations, whose interpretation crucially depends on background knowledge.

Classical Chinese Lexical Elements

There is an abundance of classical Chinese lexical elements in signs. An extraordinary example is the traffic sign below. Except for the first character 请 'please', every one of the four remaining characters is from classical Chinese!

Figure 2.1 **Please each go its way**
请各行其道 qǐng gè xíng qí dào
Compare the spoken Chinese version: 请每(辆车都)在自己的车道上走.

There are of course exceptions to this prevalence of classical words in signs. But exceptions do seem to prove the rule. Those signs using the colloquial style are generally designed deliberately to flout the convention to achieve some special effect. In learning to read signs, one can acquire the most frequently used classical Chinese lexical elements in modern Chinese contexts. A few classical words are found in the following signs.

Figure 2.2 **No person sell ticket**
无人售票 wú rén shòupiào
This is on a conductor-less bus. 无 is classical Chinese for 没有；售 is classical Chinese for 卖.

Figure 2.3 **Wait go zone**
待行区 dài xíng qū
非机动车 fēi jīdòngchē | non-motorized vehicle
待, 行 and 非 are classical for 等, 走, 不 respectively.

Figure 2.4 **Again return head**
再回首 zài huíshǒu | look back again
好吃再回头 hǎochī zài huítóu | good eat again return head
(If delicious, come back again)
泡椒牛蛙 pàojiāo niúwā | pickled bullfrog
Interestingly, both the classical and modern versions are given here to form a contrast: 再回首 vs. 再回头. 首 is classical for 头.

Mixed Compound Words with both Classical and Non-classical Components

Mixed compounds are disyllabic compounds that consist of two components, one classical and one non-classical. Although the two components do not have to be synonymous (for example, 进行 'proceed'), the ones that have the same meaning are particularly intriguing. An example is 购买, formed with a classical 购 and a non-classical 买, both meaning 'buy'. With seeming redundancy, the *raison d'être* for their existence is their stylistic distinctness. They are stylistically distinct from both of their components which themselves are distinct from each other stylistically (classical=literary; non-classical=non-literary), forming a triple contrast: 买 vs. 购 vs. 购买.

One may expect the stylistic value of these mixed compounds to be somewhere between classical and non-classical. But such expectation is not born out by facts. Using the statistical method of correspondence analysis to visualize the two dimensions of style in written Chinese, the author shows that mixed compounds are more written in style than even their classical components (Zhang 2016, 2017). This can perhaps be felt in translation. While 买 (and possibly 购) is translated as 'buy', 购买 may best be rendered as 'purchase'.

Figure 2.5 **You already enter no smoke zone**
您已进入无烟区 nín yǐ jìnrù wúyān qū
进入 is a mixed compound, both parts having the meaning 'enter'. 入 is classical for 进.

Figure 2.6 **Pedestrian**
行人 xíngrén | walk person
等待区 děngdài qū | wait area (waiting area)
Both parts of 等待 mean 'to wait'; 待 is classical for 等.

Flouting Grammatical Rules

In addition to having classical lexical elements, signs also exhibit special grammatical characteristics, which in some cases can be traced to classical Chinese as well. All the examples here yield very few hits in the large BCC corpus with billions of words. It is possible that the corpus does not include many signs.

One example is the use of the buzzword 文明 seen everywhere in China. In addition to the usual meanings of 'civilization' and 'civilized', it can also be used in other unusual ways. The following two examples show two different usages.

Figure 2.7 **Civilization ride vehicle**
文明乘车 wénmíng chéngchē
This was in a high-speed train brochure. The translation mistake shows how signs can flout grammar rules. 文明 here is neither a noun nor an adjective; it is an adverb meaning '以文明的方式' (in a civilized manner).

Figure 2.8 **Up forward one small step**
上前一小步 shàngqián yì xiǎobù
文明一大步 wénmíng yí dàbù | civilization one large step
Signs like these are posted over urinals everywhere. In parallel with the verbal 上前 'go forward', 文明 is used as a verb 'to become civilized'.

Figure 2.9 **twenty-first-century non-mobile property**
21世纪不动产 21shìjì búdòng chǎn
服务中国 fúwù zhōngguó | serve China
源于美国 yuán yú měiguó | originate in the United States
始于1971 shǐ yú 1971 | begin in 1971
服务中国 is quite unusual (服务社会 'serving society' is more common), in contrast with the usual 为中国服务. 源于美国 and 始于1971 both use the classical preposition 于 and the classical word order of verb + prepositional phrase.

Figure 2.10 **Study Lei Feng**
学习雷锋 xuéxí léifēng
奉献他人 fèngxiàn tārén | devote other people
提升自己 tíshēng zìjǐ | elevate self
Promoted by Mao Zedong sixty years ago, 雷锋's name is still synonymous with
a model citizen. Very unusual is the use of 他人 as the direct object of 奉献, in
contrast with the usual 奉献给他人/为他人奉献. By analogy with 奉献自己
'devote self', 奉献他人 can have the opposite meaning of sacrificing others!

严肃考风考纪　建设优良学风

Figure 2.11 **Serious test discipline**
严肃考风考纪 yánsù kǎofēng kǎojì
建设优良学风 jiànshè yōuliáng xuéfēng | build fine academic style
Based on the parallelism with the verbal 建设, the adjective 严肃 must be
interpreted as a verb 'to be serious about'.

京东一下 年味到家

Figure 2.12 **Jingdong it**
京东一下 jīngdōng yíxià
年味到家 niánwèi dàojiā | new year atmosphere arrive home
京东 is the name of an e-merchant and as such should not be followed by the
verbal measure 一下. Hence 京东 is used as a verb, in the same way that the
name Google has been used.

Figure 2.13 **Speaking not loud**
言语不喧哗 yányǔ bù xuānhuá
言语 can be neither a subject nor an object but seems analyzable as a topic, which is followed by the comment 不喧哗. Topic-comment is an important characteristic of Chinese grammar.

Abbreviations

Abbreviations are extremely common in Chinese. They present a particular challenge to learners. In the abbreviating process, the meaning can become very opaque. They can also be formed in an ad hoc manner and often have a short life span. Therefore, many of them cannot be found in the dictionary. Understanding them requires background knowledge and the constant updating of knowledge base.

Abbreviations may be motivated by the need to cram increasingly more information into a limited linguistic space. Many of them end up with two syllables, the preferred syllable count in the modern Chinese lexicon.

Abbreviations come in different types. Some of them simply result from truncation. Some are abbreviated from abbreviations, resulting in further opaqueness. The hardest ones use numbers, the interpretation of which is entirely dependent on background knowledge.

Figure 2.14 **Supermarket**
超市 chāoshì
Abbreviated from 超级市场, this is more frequently used than the full form.

Figure 2.15 **Beijing satellite TV**
北京卫视 běijīng wèishì
卫视 is abbreviated from 卫星电视, which is hardly used at all.

Figure 2.16 **Nation speech**
国话 guó huà | National drama theatre
This abbreviation is quite opaque in meaning. 'National speech' is the most likely (wrong) guess if you try to glean the meaning from the component characters. The full version 国家话剧院剧场 guójiā huàjùyuàn jùchǎng can be seen below.

Figure 2.17 **National drama theater**
It is amazing that this is abbreviated to two syllables.

Figure 2.18 **High iron ride train direction**
高铁乘车方向 gāotiě chéngchē fāngxiàng
高铁 is short for高速铁路, as 地铁 is for 地下铁路.

Figure 2.19 **Inn move micro iron**
驿动微铁 yì dòng wēi tiě | e-drive micro rail
This is on a shuttle bus. The abbreviation 微 'micro' is used widely, as in 微软
'Microsoft', 微推 'micro tweet' and 微信 'wechat'. Also worthy of note is 驿动.
驿, abbreviation for roadside inn 驿站, is used because it sounds like E.

Abbreviations of Abbreviations

北京2022年冬奥会
官方合作伙伴

Figure 2.20 **Winter Olympic**
北京2022年冬奥会官方合作伙伴
běijīng 2002 nián dōngàohuì guānfāng hézùo huǒbàn
Beijing 2022 year winter Olympic meet official cooperation partner
冬奥会 is short for 冬季奥运会. 奥运会 is itself short for 奥林匹克运动会,
which is quite a mouthful. But only through this unabbreviated form can we see
the connection between the transliteration 奥林匹克 and the original
word Olympic.

浦发银行
SPD BANK

Figure 2.21 **Pudong development bank**
浦发银行 pǔfā yínháng
浦发银行 is short for 上海浦东发展银行 (Shanghai Pudong Development
Bank). 浦is in itself an abbreviation for 黄埔江 Huangpu River. 浦东means east
of the Huangpu River. It is the fast-developing financial area of Shanghai.

The most striking example of iterated abbreviations involves three steps of abbreviation.

Figure 2.22 **Child program child art**
童程童美 tóng chéng tóng měi
(children computer programming and children art)
少儿编程 shào'ér biānchéng | young child compile program
This company provides instruction to children on computer programming and computer art. The abbreviations 童程, 童美 stand for 儿童编程 and 儿童美术 respectively. Interestingly, 编程is itself abbreviated from 编写程序. The whole iterated process is thus: 编写程序➜ 编程➜程!

Abbreviations by the Numbers

One particularly opaque and fleeting type of abbreviations is headed by numbers. One good example is Sun Yat-sen's 三民主义 'three people-ism', which is from 民族 'nation', 民权 'people's right', and 民生 'people's livelihood'. In the1950s, two of the political campaigns were referred to as 三反 'three anti-s' and 五反 'five anti-s'. 三反 stand for 反贪污 'anti-corruption', 反浪费 'anti-wastefulness', 反官僚主义 'anti-bureaucracy'; 五反 stands for 反行贿 'anti-bribery', 反偷税漏税 'anti-tax evasion', 反盗骗国家财产 'anti-theft of state property', 反偷工减料 'anti-cutting corners', 反盗窃国家经济情报 'anti-theft of state economic information'. In the first decade of the new millennium, the political platform of Hu Jintao and Wen Jiabao was presented as 八荣八耻 'eight to be proud of and eight to be ashamed of'. To make sense of them, one needs to be kept abreast of what is happening in China. The following example was seen in the southeastern city of Wuxi at the end of 2019. Common to many such locally produced banners, it is quite amateurish and by no means a model of elegance!

Figure 2.23 **Carry out eight etiquettes four ceremonies**

践行【八礼四仪】jiànxíng 'bā lǐ sì yí'

争做新时代好少年 zhēng zuò xīn shídài hǎo shàonián | vie be new era good teenager

八礼bā lǐ | eight etiquettes:

仪表之礼	yíbiǎo zhīlǐ	comportment etiquette
餐饮之礼	cānyǐn zhīlǐ	eating/drinking etiquette
言谈之礼	yántán zhīlǐ	speech etiquette
待人之礼	dàirén zhīlǐ	treatment of people etiquette
行走之礼	xíngzǒu zhīlǐ	walking etiquette
观赏之礼	guānshǎng zhīlǐ	touring etiquette
游览之礼	yóulǎn zhīlǐ	sightseeing etiquette
仪式之礼	yíshì zhīlǐ	ceremony etiquette

四仪sì yí | four ceremonies:

七岁入学仪式 7 suì rùxué yíshì | seven years starting school ceremony
10岁成长仪式 10 suì chéngzhǎng yíshì |ten years growth ceremony
14 岁青春仪式 14 suì qīngchūn yíshì | fourteen years youth ceremony
18岁成人仪式 18 suì chéngrén yíshì | eighteen years adulthood ceremony

Without being spelled out, the eight etiquettes and four ceremonies would be quite opaque to outsiders. The two somewhat artificially created categories seems a clumsy attempt at symmetry, as they are based on the word 礼仪 'etiquette'.

Aliases

Public signs also include aliases for place names, knowledge of which is undoubtably important. Valued for their succinctness and literary association, monosyllabic aliases are preferred over multi-syllabic official names in many contexts, including license plates, names of highways and train routes, and names of restaurants. Except for a few that are simple abbreviations of the full forms, most are distinct in form, necessitating the need to learn them separately.

To complicate matters, there is no one-to-one correspondence between aliases and the official names. The same place name may have more than one alias. For example, 云南 can be 云 or 滇; 四川 can be 川 and 蜀; on the other hand, the same alias can also stand for different places. 宁 can be the alias for 南京; but it has also been used for the province of 宁夏.

In this section, we will mostly use automobile license plates as examples (quite a few aliases used in restaurant names can be found in Chapter 10 on eating). All license plates in China start with the mono-syllabic alias for the location where the vehicle is registered. The color is uniformly blue, except electronic vehicles, which have green license plates.

Aliases come in different types. The easiest kind is the abbreviated type, which retains part of the official name.

Figure 2.24 **Alias for Guizhou**
贵 guì 'expensive, noble, precious' stands for 贵州 guìzhōu, a Southwestern province known for its mountainous terrain.

Figure 2.25 **Alias for Ningxia**
宁 níng 'peaceful' stands for 宁夏 níngxià, a Northwestern province with a mostly Muslim population. Note however 宁 is also the alias for 南京.

Figure 2.26 **Alias for Jiangsu**
Unlike the two earlier, 苏 sū is the second syllable of 江苏 jiāngsū, the province surrounding Shanghai. Note that it does not stand for 苏州, a city in the province.

Aliases Totally Different from Official Names

Totally different from the official forms, they are harder to learn than the abbreviated type. But this type is in fact the norm.

Figure 2.27 **Alias for Hubei**
鄂 è is the alias for 湖北 húběi (lake north) province.

Figure 2.28 **Alias for Shandong**
鲁 lǔ stands for the province of 山东 shāndōng (mountain east), where the ancient kingdom 鲁国 and Confucius' hometown is located. 鲁菜 refers to one of the eight main cuisines of China. It was the cuisine of the court for the last two imperial dynasties.

Figure 2.29 **Alias for Guangdong**
粤 yuè stands for the province 广东 guǎngdōng. 粤语 yuèyǔ refers to the Cantonese language/dialect; 粤菜 yuècài refers to one of the best-loved cuisines known for its fresh ingredients and subtle flavors.

Figure 2.30 **Alias for Shanghai**
沪 hù stands for the city 上海 shànghǎi. 沪剧 hùjù refers to the local opera. The green license plate shows it is an electric vehicle.

Figure 2.31 **Alias for Fujian**
闽 mǐn stands for the province 福建 fújiàn.
闽菜 refers to the local cuisine and 闽语 is one of the main dialect families of China, known for its many archaic words.

Figure 2.32 **Alias for Anhui**
皖 wǎn stands for the province of 安徽 ānhuī. It can also be used to refer to the local cuisine.

Figure 2.33 **Beijing-Shanghai Highway**
国家高速 guójiā gāosù | national high speed
京沪高速(沪宁) jīng hù gāosù (hù níng)
Beijing-Shanghai High Speed (Shanghai-Nanjing)

Learning Outcomes

a. Gain greater awareness of classical Chinese elements in public writing.
b. Gain greater awareness of the pervasiveness of abbreviations in Chinese.
c. Gain greater awareness of aliases in Chinese.

Suggested Learning Activities

1. Give the non-classical counterparts to the classical 无, 非, 待, 行, 入, 于, 首, 售.
2. Using 标识 and 警示, search online for signs that include the classical Chinese elements 无, 非, 待, 行, 入, 于, 首, 售. Type them out and translate.
3. Abbreviate the full names of schools given in Chapter 12.
4. Find the abbreviations of government offices in Chapter 12.
5. Using 略语, search online for abbreviations and give their full forms.
6. Using 数字略语, search for abbreviations headed by numbers and give their full forms.
7. Search online for signs that include the aliases given in this chapter. Type them out and translate.
8. Give the official names for the aliases 粤, 鲁, 闽, 苏, 皖, 贵, 宁, 鄂, 京, 沪.
9. Using 菜系 'cuisine system', search online for cuisines that include aliases. Give the official names.
10. Find a map of China and put the aliases for place names where they belong.

3 Rhetorical Devices

The rhetorical devices used in a language reflect both its linguistic characteristics and the cultural patterns of its users. Due to the extensive homophony in Chinese, punning is extensively exploited. The predilection for even numbers may account for the fondness for symmetry and parallelism. The special characteristics of Chinese characters naturally lend themselves to clever exploitation of graphic shape.

As expected, rhetorical devices are seen more often in public writing such as advertisements and civic banners but less in strictly functional ones like road signs. Quite a few of the examples of punning in this chapter are for advertising purposes. Most of the civic signs in Chapter 17 exhibit parallelism.

Punning with Homophony

Due to the small syllabic inventory and short word length, homonyms abound in Chinese. Many words share the same sound. Consequently, punning, i.e., using one form to evoke two meanings, is very easy to achieve. This may explain the fondness for punning in Chinese and it has been used extensively (and sometimes too easily it seems), especially in ads and names of businesses. The Chinese term for punning is 谐音 xiéyīn 'lit. harmony sound'.

Figure 3.1 **Real heart fresh**
真心鲜 zhēn xīn xiān
This is a grocery store, where freshness (新鲜) is very important. The substitution of 新 with the homophone 心 allows the alternative grouping of 真心 to mean 'earnest'. When read rather than heard, the meaning of earnestness stands out, as the combination 心鲜 'heart fresh' does not make sense.

Figure 3.2 **Heart direction**

心方向 xīn fāngxiàng

留学 liúxué | stay study 移民 yímín | move people

Study abroad   immigration

Like the sign above, the pun lies in the homophony of 心 'heart' and 新 'new'.
A new direction is also the direction your heart desires to go in!

Figure 3.3 **Scan one scan**

扫一扫 sǎo yì sǎo

码上有礼 mǎshàng yǒu lǐ | code on have gift

码 and 马 are homophonous. 码上 'on the code' sounds like 马上 'immediately'.
'Scan it and you will have gift right away.'

Figure 3.4 **Clean plate campaign**

光盘行动 guāngpán xíngdòng

不剩饭 bú shèngfàn | no leave food 不剩菜 bú shèngcài | no leave dish

文明餐桌从我做起 wénmíng cānzhuō cóngwǒ zuòqǐ

civilized dining table from me do start

光盘 originally means 'laser disk'. But 光 can also mean 'clean' and 盘 'plate'.

Figure 3.5 **Bao miss**

包小姐 bāo xiǎojie

The shocking ad has two possible meanings. 包 can be a surname, so 包小姐 can
mean Miss Bao. But who in their right mind would simply put a name with a
phone number in an ad? More likely, 包 is intended to be a verb meaning 'to
exclusively retain a miss (for her various services)'.

Figure 3.6 **Clear true**
清真 qīngzhēn | Halal
宁夏马记 níngxià mǎ jì | Ningxia Ma's
回乡情怀 huíxiāng qínghuái | return/Muslim village sentiment
宁夏 is an autonomous region in China with a Muslim majority. 回乡 can mean
'return to village', but it can also mean homeland of the Hui Muslim people.
In this context, the latter is clearly the intended meaning.

Figure 3.7 **Foreign country**
异国yìguó | foreign country 他湘 tāxiāng | other Xiang
This is a restaurant in Boston's Chinatown. 异国他湘 sounds the same as
异国他乡, which means 'foreign country and place'. 湘 is the alias for Hunan
known for its spicy cuisine.

Figure 3.8 **Crab heaven crab earth**
蟹天蟹地 xiè tiān xiè dì
蟹天蟹地 is homophonous with 谢天谢地 'thank heavens thank earth'. This ad
shows some eaters' extreme enthusiasm about eating crabs.

Punning with Partial Homophony

Sometimes, the homophony is not total, but this does not prevent the use of punning.

Figure 3.9 **Real Kungfu**
真功夫 zhēn gōngfu

Figure 3.10 **Nutrition still steam better**
营养还是蒸的好 yíngyǎng háishì zhēngde hǎo

This restaurant chain specializes in steamed (蒸) foods, which are deemed healthier. It exploits the association between 真 'real' martial art and healthy lifestyle. Never mind that 真 zhēn is not really a homophone of 蒸 zhēng 'steamed'. But for southerners, they may really be homophonous, as 'n' and 'ng' are hard to distinguish for them.

Figure 3.11 **Steamed delicious**
蒸的美味 zhēngde měiwèi
真的健康 zhēnde jiànkāng | really healthy
Apart from the near homophony between 蒸 and 真, 'steamed' and 'really' can trade places and it still makes sense: 真的美味 'really delicious', 蒸的健康 'steamed is healthy'.

Figure 3.12 **Journey purchase**
途购tú gòu
This shop selling travel accessories has a rather ingenious name. Not only do the meanings of English and Chinese match, but the Chinese name also sounds almost identical to the English one (albeit with tones).

Figure 3.13 **Come go flush flush**
来去冲冲 láiqù chōngchōng
This reminder reminds people of the phrase
来去匆匆 'come and go in a hurry'. 冲 chōng and
匆 cōng are near homophones. Their association
implies that even if you are in a hurry, you should
flush the toilet.

Figure 3.14 **Rent eight borrow**
租八借 zū bā jiè
单车出租站 dānchē chūzū zhàn | single vehicle out rent station
This is a bike rental in Taiwan. 租八借 is both a pun and an allusion to the
classic 西游记 'Journey to the West', in which the traveling entourage included
猪八戒 zhūbājiè the piggy, which sounds like 租八借 zūbājiè, especially to
southerners, who find it difficult to distinguish the retroflex zhu from the non-
retroflex zu. The allusion is easy enough for native speakers, who may have
grown up with the story, but it could be quite baffling to non-native learners.

Clever Exploitation of Graphic Shape of Characters

Due to the special nature of the Chinese script, it is no surprise that the
graphic shape of Chinese characters has been cleverly exploited.

Figure 3.15 **Hot to touch**
烫 tàng
This warning was found on the table of a Yunnan restaurant serving piping hot rice
noodles (过桥米线). Cleverly, it uses two colors for the two components of the
character. The red at the bottom is the fire radical, certainly relevant to being hot.
The blue on top 汤 is a sound clue tāng, its original meaning 'soup' not directly
related to 'hot to touch'. But here, what is hot is exactly a soup, thus highlighting
the components serves to bring out the double meaning: 汤烫 'soup is hot'!

Figure 3.16 **Warm warm and slow slow**
暖暖和缓缓 nuǎnnuan hé huǎnhuan
一直希望有两个女朋友 yìzhí xīwàng yǒu liǎnggè nǚpéngyǒu
always hope have two female friend
一个叫暖暖一个叫缓缓 yígè jiào nuǎnnuan yígè jiào huǎnhuan
one call warm warm one call slow slow
Note the similarity in both the pronunciation (nuǎn and huǎn, which rhyme) and
the shape of the two characters 暖 and 缓, sort of visual rhyming! Note the mixture
of simplified and traditional characters.

Figure 3.17 **Gallop gamy savory**
犇羴鱻 bēn shān xiān
This is the name of a restaurant in Qufu, Confucius' hometown. All three characters
are formed by three copies of the same character 牛 'ox' 羊 'sheep' 鱼 'fish'.

木木夕木目心

Figure 3.18 **Wood wood dusk wood eye heart**
木木夕木目心 mù mù xī mù mù xīn
This store sign is a clever decomposition of 梦想 'dream'. The resulting string
sounds rather nice!

Mr.FIVE 伍氏

Figure 3.19 **Wu's**
伍氏 wǔ shì
This is a store. 伍 is a family name and 氏 is used after a family name to mean
''s'. The English translation and the logo cleverly make use of the fact that 伍 can
also mean the number 5 written in 大写 (capitalized form).

Figure 3.20 **I want to love her/him just like she/he loves me**
我要像她/他爱我一样，爱她/他 wǒ yào xiàng tā ài wǒ yíyàng, ài tā
This insurance ad seen in the Beijing metro makes use of the total homophony
and partial visual similarity between the two third-person pronouns. 她/他 are
pronounced the same way and only differ in having different radicals on the left.

Symmetry and Parallelism

The Chinese predilection for even numbers may explain the indulgence
in parallelism and symmetry in public writing. The Chinese term for
parallelism is 对仗 duìzhàng. The fondness for parallelism has had a
long history, as exemplified by the excessive attention to formal symmetry in 骈文 'parallel prose' started in the Qin and Han dynasties.
Widely seen in spring couplets, civic and political banners, parallelism
can even be seen in more mundane domains such as advertisements and
restaurant menus.

Figure 3.21 **A cup of tea**
阅读 yuèdú | read 香茗 xiāngmíng | fragrant tea 聚会 jùhuì | gathering
一个人 yígè rén | a person
一本书 yìběn shū | a book
一杯茶 yìbēi chá | a cup of tea
一段回忆 yíduàn huíyì | a memory
In the second line, the uniform pattern '一 + measure word + noun' is repeated
four times, with four different measure words and four different noun phrases.
Both simplified (1st line) and traditional (2nd line) characters are used.

Figure 3.22 **Beauty at river south water**

美在江南水 měi zài jiāngnán shuǐ

食在王兴记 shí zài wáng xīng jì | food at Wang Xing's

This is found on the wall of the restaurant whose name is in the calligraphic scroll. The parallelism lies in having the same number of characters for both lines, the use of the same character 在 at the second position in both lines and following the same grammatical pattern: noun + 在 + location.

Figure 3.23 **Today divide one divide**

今天分一分 jīntiān fēnyìfēn | give it a sorting today

明天美十分 míngtiān měishífēn

tomorrow beautiful ten portion (much prettier tomorrow)

This is to urge people to sort trash. The presence of both parallelism and variation is unmistakable. The second and last characters of each line 天 and 分 are identical; the first and the fourth character of each line are different words of the same category, 今 vs. 明 and 一 vs. 十. The middle characters of both lines are verbs: 分 'divide' and 美 'beautiful'.

Figure 3.24 **Fresh shrimp talent person small wonton**

鲜虾才子小馄饨 xiānxiā cáizǐ xiǎo húntun

蟹粉佳人小馄饨 xièfěn jiārén xiǎo húntun

crab yolk beauty person small wonton

It is quite remarkable that parallelism is seen even here. The male 才子 'talented person' in the shrimp wonton matches the female 佳人 'beauty person' in the crab roe wonton.

Figure 3.25 **Donkey meat bun**
驴肉火烧lǘ ròu huǒshāo 肯得驴 kěndé lǘ | Kentucky donkey
人吃驴肉健康长寿 rén chī lǘròu jiànkāng chángshòu
people eat donkey meat healthy long life
驴吃百草浑身是宝lǘ chī bǎicǎo húnshēn shì bǎo
donkey eat hundred grass whole body treasure
天天新鲜 tiāntiān xīnxian | every day fresh
美味食品 měiwèi shípǐn | delicious food
This is on a wrapper for a 'donkey burger', a specialty of Hebei province. The
format is almost like a couplet, with a four-character horizontal line on top and
two pairs of vertical lines, which match in number of characters and structural
patterns. Note the sly allusion to KFC.

Couplets

Spring couplets 春联 chūnlián are so named because they are often put
up around the lunar new year and they come in pairs of vertical lines of
mostly seven characters, along with a horizontal line typically with four
characters. Traditionally, the horizontal line is read from right to left and
the right vertical line before the left. The most notable feature is symmetry and mirroring and contrast between words of the two vertical
lines in meaning and parts of speech.

In Figures 3.26–3.30, a few different variations of the form are given.

Figure 3.26 **Couplet 1**
富贵平安 fùguì píng'ān | wealth distinction peace
年年如意财进门 niánnián rúyì cái jìnmén
year year as wish wealth enter door
天天开心福到家 tiāntiān kāixīn fú dàojiā
day day open heart blessing arrive home
The top horizontal line should be read from right to left. Accordingly, the right vertical line should be read first. The parallelism between the two vertical lines is seen in:

1. having the same number of characters
2. repeating the first character
3. the first four characters follow the pattern: noun+noun+verb
4. the last three characters follow the pattern: subject+verb+location
5. the first four characters and the last three characters can stand alone

Figure 3.27 **Couplet 2**

万事如意 wànshì rúyì | ten thousand matter as wish (everything as you wish)
迎新春四季平安 yíng xīnchūn sìjì píng'ān | greet new spring four season peace
贺佳节五福临门 hè jiājié wǔfú línmén | congratulate fine festival 5 blessing arrive door
Even though the characters are in traditional style, the format is not entirely
traditional, the top line being read from left to right instead of right to left.
Accordingly, the vertical line on the left should also be read first. The
obligatory parallelism between the two vertical lines is seen in the
following ways:

1. both lines can be divided into two parts: three characters+four characters
2. the three-characters part in both lines has the structure verb+adj. noun.
3. the four-characters part in both lines has the structure number+noun
   +verb phrase
4. the first three characters and the last four characters can stand alone

Figure 3.28 **Couplet 3**

平安如意年年好 píng'ān rúyì niánnián hǎo
peace as wish year year good
人顺家和事事兴 rénshùn jiāhé shìshì xīng
people smooth family harmony matter matter prosperous
Even though there is no horizontal line to use as guide, the two
lines should be read from right to left. The parallelism is seen in
repeating the fifth character in both lines. In addition, the last
three characters of each line follow the same pattern: noun+
noun +adjective.

Figure 3.29 **Couplet 4**

一顺百顺万事顺 yíshùn bǎishùn wànshì shùn
1 smooth 100 smooth 10,000 matter smooth
千福万福满堂福 qiānfú wànfú mǎntáng fú
1k blessing 10k blessing full house blessing
The left line should be read first, as the number one 一 should precede one
thousand 千. Note the repetition of the two characters 顺 and 福 three times.
In the center one big 福 is accompanied by ninety-nine smaller ones in all the
variant forms, making up exactly 100 福 characters.

Figure 3.30 **Couplet 5**
迎送远近通达道 yíngsòng yuǎnjìn tōngdá dào
greet see off far near through reach path
(All paths near and far can take you here or away.)
进退迟速游逍遥 jìntuì chísù yóu xiāoyáo
forward back tardy speedy wander leisure
(However you move, do it in a carefree manner)
The left line should be read first. It is obvious that the component '辶' is common to all fourteen characters. It is not hard to come up with characters having the same component; what is challenging is to come up with two lines that still make sense and are even related in meaning.

Learning Outcomes

a. Gain greater awareness of the extent of homophony in Chinese.
b. Gain greater awareness of the prevalence of parallelism in public writing.
c. Gain greater awareness of the rhetorical potential of character components.

Suggested Learning Activities

1. Using the term 谐音, search online for more examples of punning.
2. In Chinese mode, type in 'shi' and count the number of homophonous characters.

3. In Chinese mode, type in 'qing' and write out characters with the phonetic component 青.
4. Design a sign with a pun.
5. Find examples of parallelism in Chapter 17 and explain how the parallelism works.
6. Using the term 对仗, search online for more examples of parallelism.
7. Using 春联 and 对联, search online for more examples of couplets. Identify features of parallelism in them.
8. Using 年年好, and 家和人和, search online for lines of couplets which match up with 年年好 and 家和人和 respectively.
9. Design a couplet.
10. Decompose the character 聽 and 赢 into components.

4 Non-Uniform Format

Reflecting the changes that Chinese writing has undergone during the last century, Chinese signs are neither uniform in character style nor text orientation. The mixing of different formats is also evident.

Traditional and Simplified Characters

Two kinds of Chinese characters are presently in use: traditional and simplified. While in mainland China, simplified characters have been used since the late 1950s, traditional characters are still the norm in Taiwan, Hong Kong, Macau, and most overseas communities.

It needs to be stated that not all characters have been simplified. Of the characters that have been, many correspond regularly to their traditional counterparts by having regularly simplified components such as 言>讠 ; 鳥>鸟; 馬>马; 魚>鱼.

Although most of the signs in this volume were collected from mainland China, where simplified characters enjoy official status, traditional characters are still more often seen than expected. They can be spotted on store signs, business cards, and especially calligraphy. They are apparently chosen for non-functional reasons. They convey an impression of tradition, learnedness, and general gravitas absent from simplified characters.

Figure 4.1 **Grand Gateway Office Tower**
港汇中心一座 gǎnghuì zhōngxīn yí zuò | Hong Kong assemble center 1 tower
恒隆广场 hénglóng guǎngchǎng | Henlong square
The Grand Gateway Complex is in Xujiahui district Shanghai. What's interesting is the use of both traditional characters (on the left) and simplified ones (on the right). It turns out that the 恒隆 real estate company is from Hong Kong, where traditional characters are standard. The character 港 in the name probably stands for 香港 'Hong Kong'.

Figure 4.2 **Green/red peppers**
青灯笼椒 qīng dēnglóng jiāo | green lantern pepper
红色灯笼椒 hóngsè dēnglóng jiāo | red color lantern pepper
It is amazing that green pepper is in simplified characters and the red in traditional characters. This is seen in Auckland New Zealand.

Text Orientation

As seen in old newspaper headlines, text lines traditionally were either vertical or horizontal from right to left. While vertical lines are still common, the right-to-left format has mostly been phased out except in Taiwan where they co-exist with the new left-to-right format.

Figure 4.3 **West sheep market**
西羊市 xī yáng shì
Not only is the line read from right to left, the classical Chinese word for market 市 is used. In modern Chinese it is 市场. This is in the Muslim quarter of the ancient capital Xi'an.

Figure 4.4 **Activity center**
活动中心 huódòng zhōngxīn
This should be read from right to left. This is in a University in Taiwan.

Figure 4.5 **Christian gathering place**

基督徒聚会处 jīdūtú jùhuì chù

The name of this Christian church in Taiwan is written in two traditional formats, vertically and horizontally from right to left. The biblical passages on the side walls are also presented in vertical lines, moving from right to left. All the characters are in the traditional style.

Figure 4.6 **National history museum**

国立历史博物馆 guólì lìshǐ bówùguǎn

This is a good example of the transition from the traditional to the modern format. The name of the museum (on top) is the only line that should be read from right to left, while all others are in the modern left-to-right format.

Figure 4.7 **All formats**

时代语文 shídài yǔwén | Times language

科见美语 kē jiàn měiyǔ | Kejian American language

永久国际专案管理 yǒngjiǔ guójì zhuān'àn guǎnlǐ

Forever international case management

通律法律事务所 tōnglǜ fǎlǜ shìwùsuǒ| general law office

All the possible formats are exemplified here. The topmost horizontal one is read from right to left; the two below with the same text are in both left-to-right and vertical formats; the two at the bottom are both read from left to right. This is seen in Taiwan.

Figure 4.8 **Peach garden commune**

This store in Shanghai really has outdone itself to be creative by using all possible formats, vertical and horizontal, right to left and left to right. The main sign at the top should be read from right to left as 桃园公社 táoyuán gōngshè 'peach garden commune'. But the truly crucially informative part on the top right is in the normal left-to-right format: 家具 jiājù 'furniture' 家居 jiājū 'home living' (cleverly, 家具 and 家居 use two tonally different second characters). The four characters at the bottom left are still different, in the same format as in traditional books, vertically by character and right to left by line: 桃源茶社. 源 yuán 'source' is homophonous with 园 on top and 茶 chá 'tea' replaces the 公 on top.

Learning Outcomes

a. Know where traditional characters are used.

b. Know how traditional characters are simplified.

c. Be able to identify right-to-left text orientation.

Suggested Learning Activities

1. Find ten signs in Chapter 19 in traditional characters. Where are these signs from?

2. Find five signs in Chapter 19 in right-to-left format. Where are these signs from?

3. Using 书法, search online for five pieces of calligraphy in traditional characters.

4. Using 名片, search online for five business cards in traditional characters from China.

5. Using 简化字, search online for ten characters that are regularly simplified. Write out both traditional and simplified characters.

6. Using Google Translate or other apps, convert ten signs in Chapter 19 (the Chinese diaspora) into simplified characters.

Part II
Essential Signs

5   Airport and Arrival

For many visitors to China, airports may be where Chinese signs are first seen. This chapter will sample some signs that are commonly seen at airports, including those for customs, terminals, departure lounges, boarding gates, baggage reclaims, and transportation options. Most of the airport signs are bilingual with English translations. Therefore, only the character-by-character glosses will be given.

Most of the signs in this chapter are seen at the Pudong International Airport in Shanghai.

Figure 5.1 **International arrival**
国际港澳台到达 guójì gǎng ào tái dàodá
international Hong Kong Macau Taiwan arrive reach
港澳台 are abbreviations for 香港, 澳门 and 台湾 respectively. Note even though Hongkong and Macau have been returned to China, they are still grouped together with Taiwan and foreign countries.

Figure 5.2 **Foreigners**
外国人 wàiguórén | outside country person
Does 'foreigner' sound as bad as 'alien' used in some countries?

Figure 5.3 **Customs**
中国海关 zhōngguó hǎiguān
middle country sea pass

Figure 5.4 **To terminal**
至 zhì | to
航站楼 hángzhànlóu | navigate station building
至 is classical for到 (note its left component 至).

Figure 5.5 **Distance and time to boarding gate**
至登机口距离及时间 zhì dēngjīkǒu jùlí jí shíjiān
to board airplane opening distance and time
至 and 及 are classical Chinese for 到 and 和
respectively. 口 'opening/mouth' is used for 'gate'.

Figure 5.6 **Domestic departures**
国内出发 guónèi chūfā
country inside out dispatch
内 is classical for 里 'inside'. But 国里 is
not possible.

Figure 5.7 **Self check-in**
自助值机 zìzhù zhíjī
self-help duty airplane
(self check-in)
值 seems abbreviated from 值日 'be on duty'

Figure 5.8 **First-class lounge**

69号头等舱候机室

69 hào tóuděngcāng hòujīshì

69 number head class cabin wait airplane room

候 is classical Chinese for 等. But 等机室 is not said. It is also used in 候车室.

行李检查室
Baggage Check Room

Figure 5.9 **Baggage check room**

行李检查室 xínglǐ jiǎncháshì

Figure 5.10 **Baggage claim**

领取行李 lǐngqǔ xínglǐ | claim get baggage

国内转机 guónèi zhuǎnjī | country inside transfer airplane

Figure 5.11 **Rendezvous point**
会合点 huìhé diǎn | meet join point

Figure 5.12 **Metro/maglev**
地铁 dìtiě | earth iron
磁浮 cífú | magnet float

Figure 5.13 **Taxi**
出租车 chūzūchē | out rent vehicle
There is also a loanword from English 'taxi' 的士. In Taiwan it is also called 计程车 'calculate distance vehicle'.

Figure 5.14 **Terminal shuttle bus**
航站楼摆渡车 hángzhànlóu bǎidùchē
navigate station building ferry vehicle
This is one of the ways to say shuttle bus.

Figure 5.15 **Shuttle bus**
穿梭巴士 chuānsuō bāshì
巴士 is a loanword from English. The Chinese word is 公共汽车 or 公车 for short. This is another way to say shuttle bus.

Figure 5.16 **Local bus**
市内巴士 shìnèi bāshì
city in bus
Note 内 is used, not 里.

Figure 5.17 **Airport bus tickets**
机场巴士售票处 jīchǎng bāshì shòupiàochù
airplane field bus sell ticket place

Figure 5.18 **To Downtown**
往市区方向 wǎng shìqū fāngxiàng
toward city area direction

Figure 5.19 **Parking**
停车库 tíngchē kù | stop car garage
This is covered parking, distinct from 停车场 'parking lot'.

Figure 5.20 **Airport hotel**
机场宾馆 jīchǎng bīnguǎn
airplane field guest house

Figure 5.21 **Economy cabin**
经济舱 jīngjìcāng
United Airlines is 美联航 měi liánháng, which is short for 美国联合航空公司.

Learning Outcomes

a. Gain familiarity with Chinese signs related to air travel.
b. Gain greater awareness of classical Chinese words in public signs.

Suggested Learning Activities

1. Using 机场, 航站楼, 候机, 出发, 登机, 行李, and 机场交通, search online for airport signs. You can combine the keywords with specific locations. Type out the signs.
2. Using traditional characters of the keywords, search for signs from regions outside China.
3. What do the classical words 内, 至, 候, 售, 及, 室, 处 mean? Give the non-classical counterparts.
4. Identify the classical Chinese elements 内, 至, 候, 售, 及, 室, 处 in found signs.
5. If you can, visit an airport in a Chinese-speaking area and take pictures of signs and annotate them.
6. Use the words from signs in this chapter in a written narrative about your arrival or departure from an airport in a Chinese-speaking area.

6 Hotels

It is important to bear in mind that hotels and hostels are only infrequently straightforwardly referred to as places of lodging such as 旅馆 or 旅店. They can be misleadingly called 酒店 'alcohol shop' or 饭店 'food shop'. In this chapter, only a few hotel and hostel signs will be given. They by no means exhaust all the possible ways in which hotels are named.

Figure 6.1 **Wenhai ecology hotel**
文海生态旅馆 wénhǎi shēngtài lǚguǎn
This one is called a 旅馆, a plain and unambiguous term to refer to hotels, but it is one of the least commonly used terms.

Figure 6.2 **Lake light fashion stylish hotel**
潭晖时尚风华旅店 tánhuī shíshàng fēnghuá lǚdiàn
Like 旅馆, 旅店is not misleading, but like 旅馆 it is also not the most commonly used term to refer to hotels. 潭 'pond' refers to the lake日月潭 (Sun Moon Lake), a scenic area in Taiwan.

Figure 6.3 **Beiping international youth travel lodge**
北平国际青年旅舍 běipíng guójì qīngnián lǚshè
旅舍 is not common either. Note Beijing is spelled in the old way as Peking.
A former name of the city 北平 'north peace' is also used.

Figure 6.4 **Fast speedy guest house**
快捷宾馆 kuàijié bīnguǎn
Despite its haute sounding literal meaning (宾 is used in 贵宾 'VIP') and a
somewhat elevated status in mainland China (at least it used to be so), 宾馆 is
interpreted rather differently in Taiwan with some hint of seediness.

Figure 6.5 **Like home alcohol shop**
如家酒店 rújiā jiǔdiàn
As is obvious, this is not a bar, even though it is called 酒店 'alcohol shop'. The
misleading name, which probably originated in Hong Kong, only started to be
used in mainland China in the 1980s to refer to fancier hotels.

Figure 6.6 **Purple jade food store**
紫玉饭店 zǐyù fàndiàn
As misleading as 酒店 is, the main meaning of 饭店 is hotel and not restaurant.
To make it more confusing, while 酒店 cannot be a bar, 饭店 can indeed be a
restaurant! Note the right-to-left text orientation, befitting its traditional
courtyard setting.

Figure 6.7 **Taipei teacher meeting place**
台北教师会馆 táiběi jiàoshī huìguǎn
会馆 can also mean gathering place for people from the same place or profession. Or it can refer to exclusive clubs.

Figure 6.8 **People dwelling**
民宿 mínsù
This is similar to a bed and breakfast.

Figure 6.9 **Floral Qinyuan Inn**
花筑沁园客栈 huāzhù qìnyuán kèzhàn
The somewhat quaint 客栈 is chosen to suggest old-time charm. This courtyard-style hotel is in Lijiang, a major tourist destination in Southwest China.

Figure 6.10 **Rest room**
休息房 xiūxi fáng
98 元/三小时 98 yuán/sān xiǎoshí
98 RMB/3 hours
Note this is not a 'restroom'!

Learning Outcomes

a. Gain familiarity with names of hotels and hostels.
b. Gain awareness of ambiguity in terms referring to hotels and restaurants.

Suggested Learning Activities

1. Use all possible words for hotels and hostels to look up examples online. Type out and translate the signs. Comment on their differences.
2. Use traditional characters to look up examples of hotels and hostels outside mainland China and make comparisons. Type out and translate the signs.
3. Using the terms for hotels and hostels given in this chapter, look them up in a corpus (for example, the BCC corpus http://bcc.blcu.edu .cn/) and compare their frequencies of occurrence. What is the most frequently used term and what is the least frequently used?
4. Which word in this chapter can refer to both restaurants and hotels?
5. Find similarly misleading names of restaurants in Chapter 10.

7 Basic Services

What are basic services? Apart from the need for food and shelter, getting hydrated (and duly performing 'bodily function'), getting connected and having access to funds may rank high.

Places for 'Bodily Function'

Like other languages, there are quite a few terms (including different euphemisms) for toilet in Chinese. The ones sampled here are by no means exhaustive.

Figure 7.1 **Public toilet**
公共厕所 gōnggòng cèsuǒ
In speech, 公共厕所 may be abbreviated into 公厕 or simply referred to as 厕所.

Figure 7.2 **Public toilet**
公厕 gōngcè
This is abbreviated from 公共厕所. Note the traditional character for 厕 is slightly different.

Figure 7.3 **Wash hand room**
洗手间 xǐshǒujiān
This is one of the many euphemisms for 'toilet', as is the English translation 'restroom'.

Figure 7.4 **Male hygiene room**
男卫生间 nán wèishēng jiān
卫生间 is another euphemism for 'toilet'.

Figure 7.5 **Outhouse**
茅房 máofáng | thatched house
Although the term may still be used in rural areas, few if any toilets are actually called 茅房. This is seen at a tourist spot in Taiwan, and it is clearly trying to suggest rustic charm.

Figure 7.6 **Hygiene paper**
卫生纸 wèishēng zhǐ
This is along the same line as the euphemism for toilet 卫生间.

Getting Hydrated

Figure 7.7 **Drinking water**
饮用水 yǐnyòng shuǐ | drink use water
Note classical 饮 is used instead of 喝 for 'to drink'. It is also used in compounds like 饮料 and 饮品. But unlike in Cantonese, it cannot be used by itself for 'to drink'.

Figure 7.8 **Direct drink water**
直饮水 zhí yǐn shuǐ
A relatively new thing, water from these fountains can be drunk directly
without boiling.

Courtesy Amenities

Figure 7.9 **Mother baby room**
母婴室 mǔ yīng shì
公园办公室内 gōngyuán bàngōngshì nèi
public garden office inside (inside park office)
母 and 婴 are abbreviated from 母亲 and婴儿
respectively. 内 is classical for 里.

Figure 7.10 **Baby chair**
宝宝椅 bǎobao yǐ
This is a booster chair seen in a Shanghai restaurant.

Figure 7.11 **Accessible elevator**
无障碍电梯 wú zhàng'ài diàntī
no obstacle electric ladder
无 is classical for 没有.

Figure 7.12 **Priority seating**
爱心专座 àixīn zhuānzuò
love heart special seat
Note the different ways the same concept is expressed.

Figure 7.13 **VIP seat**

重点旅客 zhòngdiǎn lǚkè | heavy point travel guest (VIP traveler)

专用座席 zhuānyòng zuòxí | special use seat

Seen on a high-speed train, the juxtaposition of 重点 and 旅客 is somewhat jarring, as 重点 is mostly used for institutions or projects such as 重点中学 'key middle school' and 重点项目 'key project'.

Figure 7.14 **AC on**

空调开放 kōngtiáo kāifàng | air condition open release

欢迎光临 huānyíng guānglín | welcome 请进 qǐngjìn | please enter

空调 is the same as 冷气 'cold air' in Hong Kong and Taiwan.

Figure 7.15 **Smoking allowed**

允许吸烟 yǔnxǔ xīyān

allow inhale smoke

Getting Connected and Charged Up

Figure 7.16 **Free Wi-Fi**

免费无线上网 miǎnfèi wúxiàn shàngwǎng

Exempt fee no wire go on network

Figure 7.17 **Free Wi-Fi**
免费网络 miǎnfèi wǎngluò
Exempt fee network

Figure 7.18 **Already with Wi-Fi coverage**
无线网络已覆盖 wúxiàn wǎngluò yǐ fùgài
No wire network already cover
账号 zhànghào | account number
密码 mìmǎ | secret code
Note the string of 8s for the password! The number 8 bā is an auspicious number
due to its sounding like 发 fā 'get rich'.

Figure 7.19 **China mobile**
中国移动 zhōngguó yídòng
This is one of the largest cellphone providers in
China. 移动 is short for 移动电话 'mobile phone'.

Figure 7.20 **China Unicom**
中国联通 zhōngguó liántōng
China United Communication
联通 is short for 联合通讯 'united communication'.

Figure 7.21 **Special SIM card vendor**
卡号专卖 kǎhào zhuānmài
card number special sell

Figure 7.22 **Public telephone**
公用电话 gōngyòng diànhuà | public use electric speech

Figure 7.23 **Public telephone**
公共电话 gōnggòng diànhuà | public share electric speech
Increasingly, these old-style phone booths have been re-purposed. Many have a Wi-Fi sign on them.

Figure 7.24 **Charger socket**
充电插座 chōngdiàn chāzuò
fill electricity plug base

Figure 7.25 **Power outlet**
电源插座 diànyuán chāzuò | electricity source plug base
Note the voltage for China is 220v, which is double that of 110v in the United States. Most computer and phone accessories, however, can now accept both 110v and 220v.

Figure 7.26 **EV charging station**
电动汽车充电站
diàndòng qìchē chōngdiàn zhàn
electric car charging station
Many electric vehicles are now seen on Chinese streets.

Banks and Banking

Figure 7.27 **Bank of China**
中国银行 zhōngguó yínháng | China silver firm
Note the use of 银 'silver' to refer to money

Figure 7.28 **China industry commerce silver firm**
中国工商银行 zhōngguó gōngshāng yínháng

Figure 7.29 **China construction silver firm**
中国建设银行 zhōngguó jiànshè yínháng

Figure 7.30 **Communication silver firm**
交通银行 jiāotōng yínháng
More than 100 years old, it is the fifth largest bank in China.

Figure 7.31 **Shanghai silver firm**
上海银行 shànghǎi yínháng

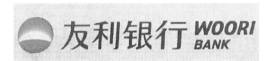

Figure 7.32 **Friend benefit silver firm**
友利银行 yǒulì yínháng
This is the second largest bank in Korea. It can be found in Chinese cities where Koreans live.

Figure 7.33 **Chase bank**
大通银行 dàtōng yínháng | big through silver firm
This branch is in Boston's Chinatown.

Figure 7.34 **Non-cash business**
非现金业务 fēi xiànjīn yèwù
Note 金 is used for money instead of 钱 in cash 现金.
Also note the use of the classical 非 'non'.

Figure 7.35 **Exchange**
货币兑换 huòbì duìhuàn
currency exchange

Figure 7.36 **Self-help banking service**
自助银行服务 zìzhù yínháng fúwù

Figure 7.37 **Deposit/withdrawal all-in-one machine**
存取款一体机 cúnqǔkuǎn yìtǐ jī
deposit withdraw one body machine

Miscellaneous Services

Figure 7.38 **Service middle heart**
服务中心 fúwù zhōngxīn

Figure 7.39 **Food delivery**
1小时速达1 xiǎoshí sùdá | 1 hour fast arrive
饿了么 èle me | hungry?
美团外卖 měituán wàimài | Meituan out sell (Meituan take-out)
送啥都快 sòngshá dōukuài | deliver what all fast (all delivery is fast)
仅在饿了么, 美团外卖购物 (饿了么, 美团外卖 purchase only)

Figure 7.40 **Fast delivery**
快递 kuàidì
无首磅wú shǒu bàng | no head pound
(No first-pound base charge)
无and 首 are classical for 没有, 第一 respectively.

Figure 7.41 **Mail drop**
邮政信筒 yóuzhèng xìntǒng
postal administration letter cylinder
中国邮政 zhōngguó yóuzhèng
China postal administration
The green cast-iron cylindrical mail collection bin
used to be a ubiquitous sight in Chinese cities, but
it is no longer very common.

Figure 7.42 **High elegant hair salon**
高雅发廊 gāoyǎ fàláng
发 is short for 头发. This is a popular hair salon in Boston's Chinatown.

Figure 7.43 **Everyone come shave head shop**
大家来剃头店 dàjiā lái tìtóu diàn
剃头 is quite an old-style word for haircut. The more common word is 理发 'tidy up hair'. This down-to-earth barbershop is seen in Taiwan.

Figure 7.44 **Pleasing housekeeping**
悦心家政 yuèxīn jiāzhèng | please heart home admin
Domestic help is very common in China.

Learning Outcomes

a. Gain familiarity with terms of basic amenities and services.
b. Gain greater awareness of the use of euphemisms.

Suggested Learning Activities

1. Using selected key words from this chapter, search online for signs with similar content. Type out the signs and translate them.
2. Using traditional characters to search for signs from regions outside China.
3. Which amenities and services are the most important to you? Which you have not used?
4. What are the most common euphemisms for 'toilet' in your area?

8   Getting Your Bearings

This chapter includes some basic signs of location, such as exit and entry, names of cities, and streets of various sizes and styles.

Entry and Exit

Otherwise short and straightforward, they do differ in the use of classical Chinese and in the range of meanings.

Figure 8.1 **Entrance**
入口 rùkǒu | enter opening

Figure 8.2 **Entrance**
进口 jìnkǒu | enter opening

These two signs for entrance differ in the first character. One is standard usage, with the classical word 入 for 'enter'. The other one with 进 is not as common, as 进口 can also mean 'import'.
There is thus an asymmetry: while 进口 may be used for both 'entrance' and 'import', 入口 cannot be used for 'import'.

Figure 8.3 **Imported food**
进口食品 jìnkǒu shípǐn | enter opening food product
Even though 进 and 入 both mean 'enter', 入口 cannot mean 'import'.

Figure 8.4 **Exit**
出口 chūkǒu | out opening
Unlike 'enter', there is only one word for 'go out'
But like 进口, 出口 can also mean 'to export'.

Figure 8.5 **Entrance/Exit**
出入口 chūrù kǒu | out enter opening
This sign combines 出口 and 入口. Interestingly, even though 进口 can mean 'entrance', 出进口 does not seem possible. Nor is reversing 出入 possible.

Figure 8.6 **Pull**
拉 lā

Figure 8.7 **Push**
推 tuī

Both characters contain the 扌 'hand' radical, which is found in many characters denoting physical action.

City Names

There are common elements in the names of cities and regions. One of them is 州 'prefecture'. It is used both in China and in other Sino-sphere countries, such as 九州 in Japan (Kyushu) and 新义州 in North Korea (Sinuiju).

Figure 8.8 **Four city names**
苏州 sūzhōu 常州 chángzhōu
无锡 wúxī 扬州 yángzhōu

Figure 8.9 **Kowloon and Hong Kong**
九龙及香港 jiǔlóng jí xiānggǎng | nine dragon and fragrant harbor
Note classical 及 for 和 'and'. The English names are based on the Cantonese pronunciation.

Names of Roads and Streets

There are quite a few words for roads and streets, which vary depending on size, style, and region.

Figure 8.10 **Ward Road**
华德路 huádé lù
Near the former Jewish refugee area in Shanghai, this road is now called 长阳路.
Note the right-to-left text orientation.

Figure 8.11 **College Road**
大学路西段 dàxué lù xīduàn | college road west section
Note the different romanization system once used in Taiwan.

Figure 8.12 **Four roads**
金惠路 jīnhuì lù
惠源路 huìyuán lù
锡澄路 xīchéng lù
欣惠路 xīnhuì lù
It is noteworthy that 惠 appears in three of the four road names.
It seems the three roads intersect.

Figure 8.13 **People's Avenue pedestrian tunnel**
人民大道 rénmín dàdào | people big path
过街地道 guòjiē dìdào | cross street earth path
道 is synonymous with 路. 道路 is a compound word referring to roads. 大道
can also be rendered as 'boulevard'.

Figure 8.14 **Chongqing Street**
重庆街 chóngqìng jiē
莺歌镇 yīnggē zhèn | Yingge town
This is a street in the town of Yingge 'nightingale song' in Taiwan known for
ceramic production.

Figure 8.15 **North money string Hutong**
北钱串胡同 běi qiánchuàn hútòng
胡同s are narrow residential lanes in Beijing. The word is said to be Mongolian
in origin.

Figure 8.16 **Dye Cloth Lane**
染布巷 rǎnbù xiàng
This is seen in Kunming Yunnan. 巷 is one of the ways to say 'lane'.

Figure 8.17 **Qingyu Road 368 Lane**

清峪路368弄 qīngyù lù 368 lòng

弄 has a distinct regional flavor. 弄s are seen everywhere in Shanghai. Note the different word order in the Chinese. The same is true of the format of dates: larger units come first.

Figure 8.18 **People's Square underpass**

人民广场地下通道 rénmín guǎngchǎng dìxià tōngdào

people square ground below through path

地下通道 can be abbreviated into 地道.

Learning Outcomes

a. Gain familiarity with common elements in place names.
b. Gain greater awareness of the possibility of multiple meanings of the same word.

Suggested Learning Activities

1. Using 州, search online for names of cities and regions. Type them out and translate.
2. Using 美国 and 州, find out online what 州 means in this context.
3. Using 路, 街, 道, 大道, 弄, 巷, 胡同, search online for road signs. Type them out and translate.
4. Using 出口, search online for examples of both the meanings of 'exit' and 'export'.
5. Find a map of China online and identify some common elements in place names.
6. Find a map of a Chinese city online and identify some common elements in road names.

Getting Around

9

In China, getting around in and between cities is done mostly by public transportation such as bus, metro, and train. For airport signs, see Chapter 5 'Airport and Arrival'.

Trains

The train remains the most popular way for inter-city transportation.

Figure 9.1 **Sell ticket machine**
售票机 shòupiào jī
信用卡 xìnyòng kǎ | trust use card
金融卡 jīnróng kǎ | finance card
Note 金融卡 for ATM card is quite different in Taiwan from 提款卡 used in Mainland China.

Figure 9.2 **Train ticket**
检票 jiǎnpiào | check ticket
无锡站 wúxī zhàn | Wuxi station
上海站 shànghǎi zhàn | Shanghai station
二等座 èrděng zuò | second-class seat
This is a cropped image of a train ticket. The name and ID number of the passenger is not shown.

Figure 9.3 **Maglev train ticket**
上海磁浮列车 shànghǎi cífú lièchē
Shanghai magnet float train
普通票 pǔtōng piào | general ticket
Shanghai's maglev train was the first in China. Note the non-idiomatic translation
of 普通票 as 'economic class'.

Figure 9.4 **Ningbo east station**
宁波东站 níngbō dōng zhàn
Very often, 站 is dropped on train timetables.

Figure 9.5 **Train to Urumqi**
阿拉山口 ālā shānkǒu | Ala mountain pass
乌鲁木齐 wūlǔmùqí | Urumqi
普客pǔ kè | ordinary passenger
This train goes from the China/Kazakhstan border to Urumqi, the capital of
Xinjiang Uyghur Autonomous Region. 普客 is short for 普通客车, which is
slower than 特快 'special fast'.

9.6 **Train to Kunming**

kāiwǎng	drive toward	昆明 kūnmíng	Kunming
2次 cì	K9612 number	8:38 开 kāi	8:38 leave
台 yī zhàntái	one platform	上车shàngchē	board train
顺序号 chēxiāng shùnxù hào	compartment order number	

Figure 9.7 **Departure level**
出发层 chūfā céng
2F refers to the second floor.

Figure 9.8 **Waiting area**
候车区 hòuchē qū | wait train zone
候 is the classical word for 等.
But 等车区 is not said.

Figure 9.9 **Check in**
检票口 jiǎnpiào kǒu | check ticket mouth
(ticket-checking/boarding gate)

车次	终到站	开点	检票口	状态
G3164	兰州西	09:44	15	停止检票
D3060	汉 口	09:46	29	正在检票
G10	北京南	10:00	1	正在检票
G1347	长沙南	09:51	7	正在检票
G7389	衢 州	09:45	20	正在检票
G1501	南宁东	10:03	3	候车

Figure 9.10 **Train status**
车次 chēcì | train number
终到站 zhōngdào zhàn | destination station
开点 kāidiǎn | depart time
检票口 jiǎnpiào kǒu | check ticket gate
状态 zhuàngtài | status
停止检票 tíngzhǐ jiǎnpiào | stop check in
正在检票 zhèngzài jiǎnpiào | checking in
候车 hòuchē | waiting for train
Note all the destinations have 站 omitted.

Figure 9.11 **Non-reserved seat**
车厢 chēxiāng | train compartment
自由座 zìyóu zuò | free seat
This is on a high-speed train in Taiwan. 自由座 can also be referred to as 自由席.

Figure 9.12 **Make up ticket place**
补票处 bǔpiào chù
Would there be a penalty for not paying upfront?

Figure 9.13 **Exit**
出站口 chūzhàn kǒu
out station mouth

Metro/Subway

Figure 9.14 **Metro**
地铁 dìtiě | ground iron
地铁 is short for 地下铁路 (underground iron road).

Figure 9.15 **Shanghai public transportation card**
上海公共交通卡 shànghǎi gōnggòng jiāotōng kǎ
The card can be used for all kinds of public transportation.

Figure 9.16 **IC card vending/recharging**
IC卡售卡/充值 IC kǎ shòukǎ/chōngzhí
IC card sell card/charge value
IC means 'smart'. 售 is classical for 卖.

Figure 9.17 **Metro station**
地铁花园桥站 dìtiě huāyuánqiáo zhàn
ground iron flower garden bridge station
6号线 liùhào xiàn | 6 number line

Figure 9.18 **Metro station**
城站站 chéngzhàn zhàn
Interestingly, the second character in the place name 站 is the same as the word
for station. The place may have been named 城站 because there was a station
there. So, the station is now called 'station of town station'.

Figure 9.19 **Metro station**
微风台北车站 wēifēng táiběi chēzhàn
slight wind Taipei station
This is a stop of the 捷运 'speedy transport' system in Taipei.

Figure 9.20 **Entrance/ticket check**
进站检票 jìnzhàn jiǎnpiào
enter station check ticket
Even though 入口 is entrance, 入站 does not seem possible here.

Figure 9.21 **To Disney**
往迪士尼 wǎng díshìní | to Disney
往 can also be 开往 'bound for'.

Figure 9.22 **Change line**
换乘3/9号线 huànchéng 3/9 hào xiàn
change ride 3/9 number line
Note 乘 is used instead of 坐.

Figure 9.23 **Metro stop**
西藏南路 xīzàng nánlù | South Tibet Road
下一站 xià yī zhàn | down one stop 'next stop'
鲁班路 lǔbān lù | Luban Road
上一站 shàng yī zhàn | up one stop 'last stop'
南浦大桥 nánpǔ dàqiáo | South Pu Big Bridge
This is a typical way to indicate the current and adjacent stops.

Figure 9.24 **Northwest entrance**
西北口 xīběi kǒu | west north mouth
Note the difference between Chinese and English: west north vs. Northwest.

Bus, Taxi

Figure 9.25 **Long distance coach**
长途汽车 chángtú qìchē | long journey car

Figure 9.26 **Tour bus**
大巴士公司 dà bāshì gōngsī | big bus company
香港观光游 xiānggǎng guānguāng yóu | Hong Kong sightsee tour
巴士 is from English 'bus'.

Figure 9.27 **Taxi**
的士 díshì
This is from English via Cantonese. Taxi can also be 出租车 'rented car' in
mainland and 计程车 'metered car' in Taiwan.

Figure 9.28 **Bus stop**
25路 lù route 朝阳广场 cháoyáng guǎngchǎng | sun-facing square
(南禅寺 nánchán sì | south zen temple)
首班 shǒubān | first bus 末班 mòbān | last bus
堰桥 yànqiáo | Yan Bridge下站xiàzhàn | next stop: 市民广场: shìmín
guǎngchǎng | citizen square
班次间隔 bāncì jiāngé | bus interval 5-15分 fēn | minutes
This is a typical bus stop route map. 首and 末 are classical words for 第一
and 最后respectively.

Figure 9.29 **Bus fare**
分段计价 fēnduàn jìjià | divide segment calculate price (price by distance)
1元起价 1 yuán qǐjià | 1 yuan start price (starting price 1 yuan)

Figure 9.30 **Transportation options**
到达层 dàodá céng | arrival level
地铁 dìtiě | metro
公共汽车 gōnggòng qìchē | bus
出租车 chūzūchē | taxi
停车库 tíngchē kù | parking garage
2号航站楼 2 hào hángzhànlóu | terminal 2
售票处 shòupiào chù | ticket office
商业 shāngyè | business
餐饮 cānyǐn | food and drink
This is in the Hongqiao airport in Shanghai.

Driving

Figure 9.31 **Driving school**
时代驾驶 shídài jiàshǐ | era driving
This is seen in Boston's Chinatown. 驾驶 is more formal than 开车. 驾驶员 is
a driver.

Figure 9.32 **Slow**

慢 màn

车辆慢行 chēliàng mànxíng | vehicle slow go

辆 is normally a measure word for vehicles, but in 车辆, it makes a generic noun referring to vehicles in general rather than specific ones. Similar generic words formed with measure words are 纸张, 书本 etc. 行 is classical for 走.

Figure 9.33 **Stop**

停 tíng

Figure 9.34 **Parking**

停车场 tíngchē chǎng | stop vehicle field

空余 kòngyú | empty remain

停车场 tends to be open-air; covered parking garages are 停车库.

Biking

Figure 9.35 **Rental bike**
美团 APP 扫码骑行 měituán sǎomǎ qíxíng
beautiful group scan code ride proceed
(Scan and go with Meituan APP)
Shared bikes (共享单车 gòngxiǎng dānchē) are found in many cities in China.
美团 is a shopping platform. 团 is short for 团购 tuángòu 'group purchase'.
Note 骑行 with classical 行 is used.

Figure 9.36 **Walk person priority**
行人优先 xíngrén yōuxiān
Even though the classical 行 is no longer used for 'walk' (still used in Cantonese),
it is still used in compounds like 行人. This sign is seen in Taiwan.

Learning Outcomes

a. Gain familiarity with means of public transportation.
b. Gain greater awareness of classical Chinese, aliases, and abbreviations in signs for transportation.

Suggested Learning Activities

1. Name different means of public transportation. Include the ones mentioned in Chapter 5.

2. Using 车,高铁,地铁,号线,车站,售票, and 检票, search online for transportation signs. Type them out and translate.

3. Using 中国 and 火车票, search for examples of Chinese train tickets. Extract as much information as possible from one.

4. Using 車票 in traditional characters, search for train tickets from outside China. Are there any differences between them and those in China?

5. Using 地鐵, 高鐵, and 車站 in traditional characters, search for signs from outside China. Are there any differences between them and those in China?

6. Using 沪宁线 and 图, search for route maps containing the aliases 沪 and/or 宁. Which cities are mentioned?

7. What do 侯, 行, 售, 首, 末, 乘, 驾驶 mean? Paraphrase in Chinese.

8. Identify foreign elements in words for transportation.

9. Identify abbreviations of train stations names in sign #10 of this chapter.

10. List the main elements in names of bus stops in sign #28 of this chapter. They are at the end of the names.

10 Eating

This chapter deals with signs to do with eating out. They include:

1. names of restaurants
2. ordering and getting foods
3. names of dishes
4. sample menus

As is the case with hotels (see Chapter 6), many restaurants have misleading names. For example, 酒家 and 酒楼 (distinct from 酒店 'hotel') are not drinking establishments. In fact, few restaurants are straightforwardly called 饭馆 or 餐馆. 饭店 is used more for hotels than restaurants. The range of names for places to eat includes 饭店, 饭庄, 酒家, 酒楼, 餐厅, 馆, 店, 居, 厨房, 楼, 美食街, and 排档.

To sound fancy and literary, aliases for place names are often used to refer to regional cuisines instead of official full names.

Figure 10.1 **Imitate (royal) cuisine**
仿膳饭庄 fǎngshàn fànzhuāng | restaurant
This is a well-known old restaurant in Beijing. 饭庄 conveys a sense of grandness.

Figure 10.2 **Hunan Chongqing restaurant**
湘渝饭店 xiāng yú fàndiàn
This is in Bishkek, Kyrgyzstan. 饭店 is not the most common term for restaurants, as it can also mean 'hotel'. The Russian word here means 'café' in the sense of an eatery.

Figure 10.3 **Muslim dining hall**
回民餐厅 huímín canting
As a cafeteria on a college campus, the term 餐厅 may convey a sense of modesty. The pinyin spelling even looks like 'canteen' in English!

Figure 10.4 **Halal BBQ restaurant**
清真 qīngzhēn | clear true (Halal)
宝宝烤肉店 bǎobao kǎoròu diàn | baby roast meat store
In the context of eating, the term 店 refers to restaurants. This restaurant is in the Muslim Street of Xi'an.

Figure 10.5 **Ma family halal restaurant**
马家清真馆 mǎjiā qīngzhēn guǎn
In the context of eating, 馆 refers to an eating or drinking establishment. This restaurant is in San Diego, California.

Figure 10.6 **Fragrance full garden**
香满园 xiāngmǎnyuán
海鲜菜馆 hǎixiān càiguǎn | seafood dish place
The term 菜馆 seems a bit non-mainstream and may even be regional. This is seen in Boston's Chinatown.

Wine or Dine?

Instead of 饭 and 菜, many restaurants are called wine house or wine shop, which are misleading terms. While 酒楼 and 酒家 are restaurants, 酒店 is more likely to be a hotel. Interestingly, none of these three can be considered bars, which is 酒吧.

Figure 10.7 **Emperor garden restaurant**
帝苑酒楼 dìyuàn jiǔlóu
It is important to note that 酒楼 does not mean a bar!
This restaurant is in Boston's Chinatown.

Figure 10.8 **New gold gate seafood wine house**
新金门海鲜酒家 xīn jīnmén hǎixiān jiǔjiā
酒家 does not mean bar either! This seems an older term. This restaurant is also in Boston's Chinatown.

Figure 10.9 **Peace wine store**
和平酒店 hépíng jiǔdiàn
The use of 酒店 is quite unusual, which usually means hotels. But this is in Kyrgyzstan! To the left and right of the Russian word for peace МИРА are the Russian and Kyrgyz words for café in the sense of an 'eatery'.

Other Names for Restaurants

Figure 10.10 **Beijing flavor building**
京味楼 jīngwèi lóu
新品京味菜 xīnpǐn jīngwèi cài | new style Beijing flavor dish
In the context of eating, 楼 often refers to restaurants.

Figure 10.11 **No name residence**
无名居 wúmíng jū
Despite its name of 'no name', this is quite a fancy restaurant in Beijing.
In general, 居s seem to be special and traditional.

Figure 10.12 **BBQ Kitchen**
烧腊厨房 shāolà chúfáng | roast preserve kitchen
烧腊 is not quite a BBQ. It is a Cantonese specialty, featuring marinated meats roasted in the oven.

Figure 10.13 **Xi'an snack**
西安小吃 xī'ān xiǎochī
小吃 is quite a bit more modest than cuisine as translated!

Figure 10.14 **Gourmet food street**
老字号美食街 lǎozìhào měishí jiē
old establishment gourmet food street

Figure 10.15 **Gourmet stall**
美食排档 měishí páidàng
排档, also known as 大排档, is Cantonese in origin. These are informal and tend to be outdoors. Popular offerings are snacks, and local specialties. This is in Boston's Chinatown.

Figure 10.16 **Fire vehicle south station**
火车南站 huǒchē nánzhàn
滇味食肆 diānwèi shísì | Yunnan flavor eatery
滇 is the alias for 云南 the province bordering Vietnam. 食肆 is rather a quaint term.
This restaurant is on the site of the former train station on the Yunnan-Vietnam line.
The French name reflects the colonial history of Vietnam.

Figure 10.17 **Wishing-tree coffee house**
愿望树咖啡馆 yuànwàng shù kāfēi guǎn

Some Restaurants Specializing in Regional Cuisines

Aliases for place names are frequently found in the names of such restaurants. For more examples of aliases, see Chapter 2 on stylistic traits.

Figure 10.18 **Sichuan Hunan cuisine**
川湘菜 chuān xiāng cài
川 is an alias for 四川 'Sichuan'; 湘 stands for 湖南 'Hunan'. Sichuan and Hunan food is very spicy. They are two of the eight major cuisines of China.

Figure 10.19 **Zuo mother Sichuan food**
左妈蜀食 zuǒmā shǔshí
蜀 is another alias for 四川, where 蜀国 the kingdom of Shu was located.

Figure 10.20 **Gather Xiang pavilion**
聚湘阁 jù xiāng gé
湖南土菜 húnán tǔcài | lake south earth dish (Hunan rustic food)
This sign includes both the alias 湘 and the official name 湖南 for the southern
province of Hunan. The shorter alias sounds more elegant, in keeping with the
literary 'pavilion'.

Figure 10.21 **Yu flavor**
渝味 yú wèi
重庆麻辣烫 chóngqìng málàtàng | Chongqing numbing spicy hotpot
Like the sign above, this sign also includes both the alias 渝 and the official
name 重庆.

Figure 10.22 **Little Wu Yue**
小吴越 xiǎo wúyuè
江浙融合菜 jiāngzhè rónghé cài | Jiangsu Zhejiang fusion food
吴 and 越 refer to the two ancient kingdoms in the present day 江苏(江) and 浙
江(浙), two of the eight major cuisines of China.

Figure 10.23 **Rendezvous with Anhui cuisine**
皖约 wǎn yuē | Anhui date
不一样的徽菜 bù yíyàng de huī cài | not same Anhui cuisine
皖 is the alias for 安徽 province, which can be shortened to 徽. 徽菜 is one of
the eight major cuisines of China.

Figure 10.24 **South north flavor**
南北风味 nánběi fēngwèi
风味 here means 'style of food', which can also be风 by itself.

Figure 10.25 **Qi family Shaanxi cuisine**
齐家陕菜 qíjiā shǎncài
The doubling of 'a' in Shaanxi is used to indicate the third tone. Shanxi is 山西 with a first tone.

Figure 10.26 **Brimming Min tea**
溢闽茶 yì mǐn chá
闽 stands for 福建 a major tea producing province in China. In fact, the word 'tea' in several European languages is a loanword from the Min dialect. In the Min dialect, 'tea' is pronounced as te, which is the origin of the word 'tea/te' in some European languages.

Some Popular Foods

Figure 10.27 **Breakfast foods**
小桃园 xiǎo táoyuán | small peach garden
油条 yóutiáo | oil stick (fried dough stick)
豆浆 dòujiāng | bean juice (soy milk)
手工点心 shǒugōng diǎnxīn | hand work dot heart (handmade snack)
面点 miàndiǎn | flour dot heart (wheat-based snack)
Note simplified characters are used for the name of this restaurant in Shanghai, while traditional characters are used for the food items.

Figure 10.28 **Sea bottom scoop hotpot**
海底捞火锅 hǎidǐ lāo huǒguō
早9点至次晨7点 zǎo 9 diǎn zhì cì chén 7 diǎn
morning 9 o'clock to next morning 7 o'clock
This is one of the most popular hotpot chain
restaurants. Note the red chili in the logo Hi, which
sounds like 海 in 海底捞. 至 is classical for 到; 次
means 'next in line'.

Figure 10.29 **Home have good skewer**
家有好签 jiāyǒu hǎo qiān
8毛钱吃串串8 máoqián chī chuànchuan | 80 cents eat skewer stick
成都比火锅好吃的串串 chéngdū bǐ huǒguō hǎochī de chuànchuan
more delicious skewer than hotpot in Chengdu
Both extremely popular, 火锅 is usually served indoors, while 串 is a
quintessential street food.

Ordering, Picking Up, and Taking Out

Figure 10.30 **Cellphone order**
手机自助点餐 shǒujī zìzhù diǎncān
cellphone self-help order meal
点餐不排队 diǎncān bù páiduì
order meal not line queue
苗圃餐厅 miáopǔ cāntīng
nursery restaurant
扫码点餐 sǎomǎ diǎncān
scan code order meal
看屏取餐 kànpíng qǔcān
watch screen fetch meal

Figure 10.31 **(cof)fee fast**
啡快 fēi kuài
在线点 zàixiàn diǎn | online order
到店取 dàodiàn qǔ | go store get
新功能上线 xīn gōngnéng shàngxiàn | new function online
Note the pun 啡快, which retains the second syllable of coffee and sounds like 飞
快 'lightning fast'.

Figure 10.32 **Wrap up take away**
打包带走 dǎbāo dàizǒu
打包 is also used for taking away leftovers.

Names of Dishes without Cooking Verbs

A dish can be named by just listing the main ingredients, with the most
important ingredient given at the end. The shapes of the ingredients can
also be mentioned, which include 片 'slice', 块 'chunk', 丝 'thread', and
末 'minced', etc.

Figure 10.33 **Minced meat eggplant rice**
肉末茄子饭 ròumò qiézi fàn
末 'minced' is the shape of the ingredient 肉 'meat'.

Figure 10.34 **Black pepper cow meat rice**
黑椒牛肉饭 hēijiāo niúròu fàn
进店必点 jìn diàn bì diǎn | enter store must order
套餐包含 tàocān bāohán | set meal include
瓦锅饭 wǎguō fàn | clay pot rice + 酱汁 jiàngzhī | paste sauce
Black pepper is the seasoning while beef rice are the main ingredients.

Names of Dishes with Cooking Verbs

The main verbs of cooking are 炒 chǎo 'stir-fry', 烧 shāo 'braise', 煎 jiān 'sautee', 蒸 zhēng 'steam', 炸 zhá 'deep fry' and 拌 bàn 'mix'.

Figure 10.35 **Baby most love**
宝宝最爱 bǎobao zuìài
红烧狮子头饭 hóngshāo shīzitóu fàn
red braised lion head rice
狮子头 is a large meat ball. The cooking verb is 烧 'braise'. 红烧 is 'braised with soy sauce'.

Figure 10.36 **Scallion oil mix oat noodles**
葱油拌莜面 cōngyóu bàn yóumiàn
酸菜炒莜面 suāncài chǎo yóumiàn
sour vegetable stir-fry oat noodles
The cooking verbs are 拌 'mix' and 炒 'stir-fry'.

(Parts of) Menus

Figure 10.37 **Goose**

鹅肉 éròu | goose meat
米粉 mǐfěn | rice noodle
冬粉 dōngfěn | bean noodle
面 miàn | noodle
香饭 xiāngfàn | fragrant rice
This is from a night market in Taiwan. 冬粉 is Taiwanese for 粉条/粉丝 'vermicelli'.

Figure 10.38 **Fruit/melon juice**

___汁 zhī | ___juice
___果汁 guǒzhī | ___fruit juice
___瓜汁 guāzhī | ___melon juice
___牛奶 niúnǎi | ___cow's milk
This is also from a night market in Taiwan. The blanks are different fruits and melons.

Figure 10.39 **Western style hamburger**

西式汉堡 xīshì hànbǎo
汉堡 hànbǎo | hamburger
热饮 rèyǐn | hot drink
薯条 shǔtiáo | fries
鸡米花 | jī mǐhuā | popcorn chicken
奶茶 nǎichá | milk tea
咖啡 kāfēi | coffee
This menu is from the Muslim cafeteria in Capital Normal University in Beijing.
Can you figure out what kinds of burgers and milk teas are on offer?

Figure 10.40 **Farmhouse snacks**
农家小吃 nóngjiā xiǎochī
早点类 zǎodiǎn lèi | breakfast type
面类 miàn lèi | noodle type
饺子类 jiǎozi lèi | dumpling type
Can you find the four cooking verbs?

Figure 10.41 **Fast-food menu**
鲔鱼 wěiyú | tuna 可颂 kěsòng | croissant 潜艇堡 qiántǐngbǎo | sub 套餐 tàocān | set meal
嫩鸡 nèn jī | tender chicken 附fù | come with 甜品 piánpǐn | dessert 饮料 yǐnliào | beverage
牛肉 niúròu | beef 水果 shuǐguǒ | fruit 总汇 zǒnghuì | combo 三明治 sānmíngzhì | sandwich
火腿 huǒtuǐ | ham 蛋 dàn | egg 烤吐司 kǎo tǔsī | toast
Measuring words: 片 piàn | slice 个 gè | item 杯 bēi | cup
This is a Western fast-food restaurant in Taiwan. Can you match the items with the
annotations in simplified characters with those on the menu in traditional characters?

Learning Outcomes

a. Gain familiarity with names of restaurants.

b. Gain awareness of the ambiguity in terms referring to restaurants.

c. Gain awareness of the prevalent use of aliases to refer to types of cuisine.

d. Gain some familiarity with the format of names of dishes in Chinese.

Suggested Learning Activities

1. Using 酒家, 酒楼, 馆, 店, search online for names of restaurants. Type out and translate.

2. Use a corpus (for example, BCC http://bcc.blcu.edu.cn/) to look up terms referring to restaurants and eateries and compare their frequencies of occurrence. What is the most frequent and what is the least frequent?

3. Using 菜系 'cuisine system', search online for the eight major cuisines. Type out the aliases standing for the regions and give the official names of the places.

4. Identify foreign elements.

5. Order both something to eat and drink from the menu 西式汉堡 (sign #39). Total the cost. Type out the items ordered and translate them into English.

6. Find all the cooking verbs in the menu called 农家小吃 (sign #40)

7. For the menu from a Taiwanese fast-food restaurant (sign #41),
   a. name the cheapest dish on the menu; type out text and translate into English
   b. name the most expensive on the menu; type out the text and translate into English

8. Using cooking verbs such as 红烧, 炒, 拌, 蒸, search online for names of dishes.

9. Create two dish names of each of the following two types:
   a. ingredient 1+ ingredient 2
   b. (ingredient) + cooking verb + ingredient

10. Use signs in a narrative on a related topic (e.g. going to a restaurant).

Shopping

Included in this chapter are some signs seen in shopping establishments. They mainly include:

1. types of businesses
2. parts of a store, such as the cashier and the counter for writing down a sale
3. (non-cash) payment methods
4. sales and saving
5. receipts

Types of Business

Figure 11.1 **Kaiyuan mall**
开元商城 kāiyuán shāngchéng
Kaiyuan commercial town

Figure 11.2 **Year goods big street**
年货大街 niánhuò dàjiē
It is a tradition to shop for things needed for the Chinese new year 年货.

Figure 11.3 **Family harmony supermarket**
家和超级市场 jiāhé chāojí shìchǎng
The abbreviated 超市 is more common in speech.

Figure 11.4 **New prosperity food stuff**
新荣食品 xīnróng shípǐn
Sun Wing is how 新荣 is pronounced in Cantonese.
This is in Boston's Chinatown.

Figure 11.5 **Miscellaneous merchandise**
家电 jiādiàn 纺织 fǎngzhī
百货 bǎihuò 化妆品 huàzhuāngpǐn
百货 'miscellaneous merchandise' is strangely rendered as bazaar, which is really bizarre!

Figure 11.6 **Sun up exempt tax firm**
日上免税行 rìshàng miǎnshuì háng
This was seen at an airport.

Figure 11.7 **Kim Tai jewelry gold firm**
金泰珠宝金行 jīntài zhūbǎo jīnháng
It is unclear whether 'kim' is an artifact of the romanization system or due to a dialect different from Cantonese, which is more like 'kam'. This is in Boston's Chinatown.

Figure 11.8 **C-store**
喜士多 xǐshìduō | happy people much
便利店 biànlì diàn | convenience store
喜 is transliteration of C; 士多 is from English 'store'. This is a Taiwanese chain.

Figure 11.9 **Hardware**
苏北五金 sūběi wǔjīn | Jiangsu north five gold
(North Jiangsu hardware)
苏 is the alias for 江苏. Note hardware is 'five gold/metal' (五金).

Figure 11.10 **Underwear shop**
内衣店 nèiyī diàn | inner clothing shop
This is quite straightforward, a world's difference from 'intimate apparel'!

Figure 11.11 **Outdoor travel**
犟驴 jiànglǘ | stubborn donkey 旅游lǚyóu | travel休闲 xiūxián | leisure 户外hùwài | outdoor
Why is a stubborn donkey associated with travel? Because donkey (lǘ) and travel (lǚ) sound similar, diff
only in tone. Travel companions are often jocularly referred to as donkey friends (驴友).

Inside a Business

Figure 11.12 **Business hour**
营业时间 yíngyè shíjiān | do business time
对公业务 duìgōng yèwù | toward public business
个人业务 gèrén yèwù | individual business
周一至周五 zhōuyī zhì zhōuwǔ | Monday to Friday
周六, 周日 zhōuliù, zhōurì | Saturday, Sunday
节假日 jiéjià rì | festival vacation
周 is used instead of 星期; 至 is used instead of 到.
This is actually in a bank, hence the distinction between corporate banking and personal banking.

Figure 11.13 **Welcome**
欢迎光临 huānyíng guānglín
welcome illustrious arrive
Carrefour (家乐福) is a French
hypermarket chain.

Figure 11.14 **Welcome**
欢迎莅临 huānyíng lìlín | welcome attend arrive
Seen in Taiwan, this is in traditional characters and more formal than 欢迎光临.

Figure 11.15 **Open ticket center**
开票中心 kāipiào zhōngxīn
This is often the first step in making a purchase, followed by payment at the till.

Figure 11.16 **Cashier**
收银台 shōuyín tái | receive silver counter
Note the use of 银 'silver' instead of 钱. 金 'gold' is also used for money, such as 租金 'rent money'.

Figure 11.17 **Shopping card**
购物卡 gòuwù kǎ | purchase stuff card
The classical 购 is used instead of 买 for 'to buy' and 物 instead of 东西 for 'things'.

Payment Methods

In today's China, the number of non-cash payment options is staggering. They range from bank cards to cellphone apps to even face recognition. In a grocery chain owned by Jack Ma in Ningbo, the author found he had no way of paying, since he had none of the non-cash payment options.

Figure 11.18 **Payment methods**
可刷卡消费 kěshuākǎ xiāofèi | may swipe card consume
快捷新生活 kuàijié xīn shēnghuó | fast direct new life
银联支付 yínlián zhīfù | Union Pay
支付宝支付 zhīfùbǎo zhīfù | Ali Pay
微信支付wēixìn zhīfù | Wechat Pay
Note 支付 is used instead of 付钱. 宝 in 支付宝 (Ali Pay) is often used to refer to a favorite gadget, such as 充电宝 'electric charger'.

Figure 11.19 **Scan code**
立刻扫码 lìkè sǎomǎ | instant scan code
购咖啡 gòu kāfēi | buy coffee
Note 购 is used instead of 买.

Figure 11.20 **Scan once**
微信扫一扫 wēixìn sǎoyìsǎo | Wechat scan once
支付宝扫一扫 zhīfùbǎo sǎoyìsǎo | Ali pay scan once
The implied object of 扫 is 码 'code'.

Figure 11.21 **Swipe face pay**
刷脸支付 shuāliǎn zhīfù
靠脸吃饭 kàoliǎn chīfàn | depend face eat food
As 刷 is normally used with 卡, as in swiping cards, its use with 脸 is a bit amusing. Note the attempt at humor 靠脸吃饭.

Sales and Saving

Figure 11.22 **Low price**
本店同类 běndiàn tónglèi | this shop same type
低价 dījià | low price
among same type low price in this shop

Figure 11.23 **Special price**
特价 tèjià
特 is short for 特别.

Figure 11.24 **Big drop price**
大降价 dà jiàngjià
比医院更便宜 bǐ yīyuàn gèng piányi
compare hospital even cheaper

Figure 11.25 **Big reduce price**
大减价 dà jiǎnjià
减价 is similar to 降价.

Figure 11.26 **Instant reduction**
满 150元 mǎn 150 yuán | full 150 yuan
(when purchase total reaches 150 yuan)
立减lì jiǎn | instant reduce
The implied object of 减 is 价.

Figure 11.27 **Discount**
折 zhé | break
In Chinese, the number+折 (×10) refers to the percentage of the full price; but in English the percentage is the amount of discount.

Figure 11.28 **Up to 70% off**
低至三折 dī zhì sānzhé | low to three break
70% off is 30% of the full price (三折). Therefore, English is 'up to', but Chinese is 'low to'.

Figure 11.29 **Everything 90% off**
全场1折 quánchǎng 1 zhé | whole lot 1 break
Mind you, it is 90% off, not 10%!

Figure 11.30 **Half price day**
周三 zhōusān | Wednesday 半价日 bànjià rì | half price day
每周四外卖全部6折 měi zhōusì wàimài quánbù 6 zhé
every Thursday takeout everything 40% off

Figure 11.31 **Jasmine fresh flower cake**
茉莉鲜花饼 mòlì xiānhuā bǐng
买四送二 mǎi sì sòng èr | buy 4 gift 2
单个 dāngè | single one 会员价 huìyuán jià | member price

Figure 11.32 **Buy 4 get 1 free**
买 4免1 | mǎi 4 miǎn 1 | buy 4 exempt 1
(最便宜的1件免费) zuì piányi de 1 jiàn miǎnfèi | cheapest one free
免 seems less common than 送 in the expression 'buy N get N free'.

Figure 11.33 **Gifting red pouch**
送红包 sòng hóngbāo
18元代金券 18 yuán dàijīn quàn
18 yuan cash equivalent voucher

Figure 11.34 **Save even more**
省更多 shěng gèngduō
Note the Chinese yen sign at the bottom of the character 省.

Figure 11.35 **Hot sell**
热卖rè mài
Unexpectedly, 热售 with the classical word for 'sell' is much less frequent.

Figure 11.36 **Clearance sale**
清货 qīng huò | clear stock.
5 折 zhé | five break (50% off)
清仓 is more common, where 仓 cāng is warehouse.

Figure 11.37 **Best value**
最划算 zuì huásuàn
泰式南洋奶茶 tàishì nányáng nǎichá | Thai style south sea milk tea
划算 is rather colloquial, which is quite unusual. This was seen in a Chinese supermarket in San Diego, California.

Figure 11.38 **Member price**
会员尊享 huìyuán zūn xiǎng
member respect enjoy
非会员价 fēi huìyuán jià
not member price
非 is classical for 不是.

Receipts

Figure 11.39 **Fixed amount receipt**
上海公共交通卡股份有限公司
shànghǎi gōnggòng jiāotōng kǎ gǔfèn yǒuxiàn gōngsī
Shanghai public transport card limited company
国家税务总局 guójiā shuìwù zǒngjú | state tax general bureau
定额发票 dìng'é fāpiào | fix amount receipt
统一社会信用代码 tǒngyī shèhuì xìnyòng dàimǎ | standard social credit code
人民币 rénmínbì | RMB (Chinese currency)
壹佰元 yì bǎi yuán | 100 yuan
This type of fixed amount receipt is often given out by taxi drivers. Note the
more formal 壹佰 is used instead of 一百. Numbers 1–10 written this way: 壹贰
叁肆伍陆柒捌玖拾.

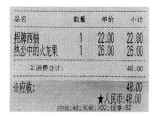

Figure 11.40 **Fruit receipt**

品名 pǐnmíng	product name
数量 shùliàng	quantity
单价 dānjià	unit price
小计 xiǎojì	sub total
消费合计 xiāofèi héjì	consumption total
应收 yīngshōu	should receive
实收 shíshōu	actually receive
找零 zhǎolíng	give change

Figure 11.41 **Fruit receipt**

商品名 shāngpǐn míng	name of merchandise
单价 dānjià	unit price
数量 shùliàng	quantity
金额 jīn'é	amount
件数 jiànshù	number of pieces
商品总价 shāngpǐn zǒngjià	total price of merchandise
订单总金额 dìngdān zǒng jīn'é	total amount order
现金支付 xiànjīn zhīfù	cash payment
实付金额 shí fù jīn'é	actuall payment amount

Note 'amount' is 金额 'gold amount' rather than 钱数.

Learning Outcomes

a. Gain familiarity with the names of commercial establishments.
b. Gain familiarity with ways to indicate discount.
c. Gain familiarity with ways of non-cash payment options.

Suggested Learning Activities

1. How many ways are there to refer to commercial establishments?
2. Using 店,商场,市场, and 购物中心,search for names of shopping establishments. Type them out and translate.
3. Using 价,打折,支付,收银,现金,金额, and 发票,search for signs related to shopping. Type them out and translate.
4. Using traditional characters, repeat the above searches for regions outside China.
5. How many ways are there to indicate discount and price reduction?
6. List all compound words containing 价.
7. How many non-cash payment methods have you not used?
8. Use signs in a narrative on a related topic (e.g. shopping).

12   Schools and Offices

This chapter includes signs from various educational institutions in mainland China and Taiwan and a few of school and government offices.

Educational Institutions at Different Levels

It is worth noting that in informal speech, abbreviated forms are used, often affectionately.

Figure 12.1 **Communication University**
交通大学 jiāotōng dàxué | communication big study
Note that 'university' in Chinese is 'big study'. Traditional characters are used, even though this is in Shanghai. The abbreviation is 交大.

Figure 12.2 **Capital Normal University**
首都师范大学 shǒudū shīfàn dàxué
head metropolis teacher model big study
Normal universities for training teachers are common in China. The abbreviation is 首师大.

109

Figure 12.3 **Campus directions**

首都师范大学 shǒudū shīfàn dàxué

学生公寓 xuéshēng gōngyù

综合楼 zònghé lóu

学生食堂 xuéshēng shítáng

外语学院 wàiyǔ xuéyuàn

The translation of 综合楼 is quite strange. Maybe a multi-purpose building?

Figure 12.4 **National Taiwan Normal University**

国立台湾师范大学 guólì táiwān shīfàn dàxué

state establish Taiwan teacher model big study

In the center of the logo on the left is the abbreviation 师大.

Figure 12.5 **National Open University**

国立空中大学台南中心 guólì kōngzhōng dàxué táinán zhōngxīn

成功大学光复校区 chénggōng dàxué guāngfù xiàoqū

Chenggong University Guangfu campus

Figure 12.6 **Taipei city Jianguo high school**
台北市立建国高级中学 táiběi shìlì jiànguó gāojí zhōngxué.
Taipei city establish build country high grade middle study
建中 in the triangular logo, read from right to left, is the abbreviation of the full
name. On closer look, the logo also incorporates the city name台北 (北 above 台).

Figure 12.7 **Beipu national elementary school**
新竹县 xīnzhú xiàn | new bamboo county
北埔国民小学 běipǔ guómín xiǎoxué
县长 xiànzhǎng | county head 郑永全 zhèng yǒngquán
题 tí | inscribe
国民小学 is often abbreviated as 国小 (国民中学 is
abbreviated as 国中). 国小 and 国中 are both compulsory
in Taiwan.

Figure 12.8 **Kindergarten**
金囡幼儿园 jīnnān yòu'éryuán
gold child young child garden
囡 is child in the Shanghai dialect.

Figure 12.9 **Mandarin training center**
国语教学中心 guóyǔ jiàoxué zhōngxīn
national language teaching center
This center is affiliated with Taiwan Normal
University, and it is the best-known institution for
teaching Chinese in Taiwan. Note the use of 国语
'national language' to refer to Mandarin Chinese.
In the center logo, the abbreviation 师大 is seen.

Figure 12.10 **Chinese language center**

华语中心 huáyǔ zhòngxīn

This center is part of the Chenggong University in Tainan. The choice of 华语 'language of ethnic Chinese' instead of 汉语 'language of Han people' or 国语 'national language' is worth noticing. The term seems to be gaining ground and it is exclusively used in Singapore.

Figure 12.11 **Library**

图书馆 túshūguǎn | graph book place

The term came from Japanese. This is the main library of Taiwan University.

Figure 12.12 **Main library**

总图书馆 zǒng túshūguǎn

This plaque is inside the main library of Taiwan University. Note the right to left orientation and the vertical lines on the sides about the alumni donors.

Figure 12.13 **Library (room)**

图书室 túshūshì | graph book room

This is the one-room library of the Mandarin Training Center of Taiwan Normal University.

Figure 12.14 **Computer classroom (2)**
电脑教室(二) diànnǎo jiàoshì (èr)

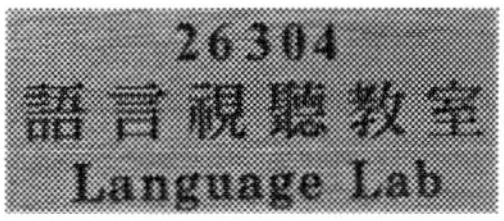

Figure 12.15 **Language visual audio classroom**
语言视听教室 yǔyán shìtīng jiàoshì

Figure 12.16 **Self-study room**
自修室 zìxiū shì
This is in the Mandarin Training Center of Taiwan Normal University.
In mainland China it will be '自习室' where 习 is short for 学习 'study'. 修 is
also used in 主修 'major' and 辅修 'minor'.

Figure 12.17 **Student lounge**
学生休息室 xuéshēng xiūxi shì | student rest room

Figure 12.18 **Office**
办公室 bàngōng shì
do business room

Figure 12.19 **Bulletin board**
校外布告栏 xiàowài bùgào lán
off-campus bulletin board

Figure 12.20 **Campus e-card information service station**
校园e卡资讯服务站 xiàoyuán e kǎ zīxùn fúwù zhàn

Figure 12.21 **Parents pickup area**
一(1) 班 yī (1) bān | 1st year (1) class
五(1) 班 wǔ (1) bān | 5th year (1) class
放学区 fàngxué qū | let out school zone
This is seen at an elementary school
in Shanghai.

Figure 12.22 **Parent pickup and drop-off zone**
家长接送区 jiāzhǎng jiēsòng qū
house head receive send zone
This is seen in Taipei, Taiwan.

Figure 12.23 **Cram class**
补习班 bǔxí bān | mend study class
These after-school classes are
extremely numerous.

Offices

Offices at different levels of the governmental hierarchy are 部, 局, 处, 科, 委, and 室.

Figure 12.24 **President's office**
院长室 yuànzhǎng shì | college head room
党委书记室 dǎngwěi shūjì shì | party committee secretary room
院 is short for 学院 'college'. 党 and 委 are abbreviations of 共产党 'communist party' and 委员会 'committee' respectively. In China, leadership at every level is shared by two nominally equal-ranking people: the communist party head side by side with the administrative head. In this instance, the president and the party secretary are one and the same person. Therefore, the two offices are in the same room.

Figure 12.25 **International exchange affairs office**
国际交流事务室 guójì jiāoliú shìwù shì
This office takes care of all matters relating to international students, and international exchanges.

Figure 12.26 **International affairs/R&D**
国际事务处 guójì shìwù chù
研究发展处 yánjiū fāzhǎn chù
This is in a university in Taiwan. 处 is a mid-level administrative unit. 研究发展 is often abbreviated as 研发 (R&D).

Figure 12.27 **International cooperation and exchange**
国际合作与交流处 guójì hézuò yǔ jiāoliú chù
护证 for room 106 is and abbreviation of 护照 'passport' and 签证 'visa'.
Note translations for room 101 and 104 are incomplete. 101 is missing the
translation for 港澳台 'Hong Kong, Macau, Taiwan' and 104 is missing that
of 自费 'self-funded'.

Figure 12.28 **Floor index**
The floor index of this government office building gives a glimpse into the
bureaucratic hierarchy. There are four types of units: 部 'department', 局
'bureau', 委 'commission', and 室 'office'. It is full of abbreviations, which can be
a bit opaque for outsiders. 发改委, located on 4F and 5F, stands for 发展改革委
员会 'development and reform commission'. A product of Reform and Opening
up started in the late 1970s, this is a relatively late comer to the Chinese lexicon.
纪委 on 10F–12F on the other hand has had a longer history. It was established
when the PRC was founded in 1949 and re-established during the Reform years.
It stands for 纪律检查委员会 'disciplinary and oversight commission'. 政研室
on 8F is abbreviated from 政策研究室 'policy research office'. 党工委 on 3F is
abbreviated from 共产党工作委员会 'party work committee'.

Learning Outcomes

a. Gain some familiarity with the terms referring to educational establishments.
b. Gain some familiarity with the terms referring to levels in bureaucracy.
c. Gain greater awareness of the use of abbreviations.

Suggested Learning Activities

1. Using 大学, 中学, and 小学, search online for educational institutions at various levels. Type out the names and translate them.
2. Using 教室, 室, and 班, search online for parts of a school. Type out the text and translate.
3. Using 部, 局, 处, 科, 委, and 室, try to find online an organizational chart of the administrative hierarchy.
4. Using traditional characters to repeat the above searches for regions outside China.
5. Abbreviate the full names of schools in this chapter.
6. Find the abbreviations of government offices in this chapter.
7. Using abbreviations, search online for educational and government institutions.

Culture and Entertainment

13

This chapter includes cultural institutions, entertainment venues, and media.

Museums

Figure 13.1 **Capital museum**
首都博物馆 shǒudū bówùguǎn
江泽民 jiāng zémín | Zemin Jiang
首都 literally is 'head metropolis'. Jiang was a former communist party boss. Note the choice of traditional characters.

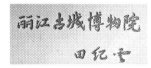

Figure 13.2 **Lijiang old town museum**
丽江古城博物院 lìjiāng gǔchéng bówùyuàn
田纪云 tiánjìyún | Jiyun Tian
Tian was a former vice premier.

Figure 13.3 **Qi Baishi old residence memorial museum**
齐白石旧居纪念馆 qí báishí jiùjū jìniànguǎn
齐白石 (1964–1957) was a famous traditional painter.

Figure 13.4 **Deyao Yu Art Museum**
余德耀美术馆 yúdéyào měishùguǎn
余德耀 (Budi Tek) is an Indonesian Chinese art collector. The museum is in Shanghai.

Figure 13.5 **Chung Yuan University Art Center**
中原大学艺术中心 zhōngyuán dàxué yìshù zhōngxīn
This university is in Taiwan.

Historical Sites

Two of the common words are 故 'former' (故址, 故城, 故居) and 址 'site' (遗址 and 旧址).

Figure 13.6 **Tang dynasty Huaqing palace royal bath former site**
唐华清宫御汤遗址 táng huáqīnggōng yùtāng yízhǐ
This is near Xi'an, the capital of Tang Dynasty.

Figure 13.7 **Qin first emperor mausoleum cultural relics display hall**
秦始皇帝陵文物陈列厅 Qínshǐhuáng dìlíng wénwù chénliè tīng
The mausoleum is near Xi'an. Note the seal style characters.

Figure 13.8 **Genghis Khan's thirty-fifth generation descendant's former residence**
成吉思汗35代世孙故居 chéngjísīhán 35 dài shìsūn gùjū
This is in Beijing, which was the capital of the Yuan Mongolian dynasty.

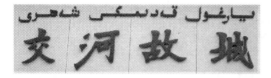

Figure 13.9 **Jiaohe old town**
交河故城 jiāohé gùchéng
This was from over 2,000 years ago. It is in Turpan Xinjiang, on the ancient Silk Road.

Temples

Two common words to refer to temples are 寺 and 庙. In fact, the generic term for temples is 寺庙.

Figure 13.10 **Longfu Temple**
隆福寺 lóngfú sì
This is the former site of a Buddhist temple in Beijing.

Figure 13.11 **Hangzhou Confucius Temple**
杭州孔庙 hángzhōu kǒngmiào

Figure 13.12 **Tainan Confucius Temple**
全台首学 quán tái shǒu xué
whole Taiwan first school
This is the largest Confucius Temple in Taiwan, located in the city of Tainan.

Figure 13.13 **Mosque**

清净寺 qīngjìng sì | clear clean temple
创建于公元1009年 chuàngjiàn yú gōngyuán
1009 nián | build in AD 1009 year
This mosque is in the coastal city 泉州. 泉州 was a
major port during the time of the Marine Silk
Road. Along with foreign merchants came many
foreign religions. 泉州 thus gained the reputation
of being 'a museum of the world's religions'.

Figure 13.14 **Ohel Moishe Synagogue**

摩西会堂旧址 móxī huìtáng jiùzhǐ |Moses
meeting hall old site
This synagogue was in the old Jewish
settlement in Shanghai.

Books

Figure 13.15 **Bao Yugang Library**

包玉刚图书馆 bāo yùgāng túshūguǎn
The late 包玉刚 was a Hong Kong shipping magnate and major
philanthropist originally from Ningbo China. Libraries bearing
his name are found in Hong Kong and mainland China. This
one is in Hong Kong and is thus in traditional characters.

Figure 13.16 **Five ring book bar**

五环书吧 wǔ huán shū bā
无线网络 wúxiàn wǎngluò | no wire net (Wireless internet)
精品图书 jīngpǐn túshū | exquisite object graph book 'fine books'
五环 seems to refer to the fifth ring road encircling outer Beijing. 吧 bā is
originally used only in 酒吧 'bar', but it has been extended to 网吧 'internet café'
and 书吧 'book café'.

Entertainment

Figure 13.17 **Wanda movie town**
万达影城 wàndá yǐngchéng
售票 shòupiào | sell ticket
This one is typical of the new style multiplex theatres. 万达 Group is a large conglomerate engaged in many lines of business. Note 售票 cannot be 卖票, even though the meaning is the same.

Figure 13.18 **Poly Theater**
保利剧院 bǎolì jùyuàn
This is a large performance venue in Beijing.

Figure 13.19 **Dream Taiji Theater**
梦幻太极剧场 mènghuàn tàijí jùchǎng
This is in a theme park in 横店, the movie studio town in Zhejiang province.

Figure 13.20 **Xi'an concert hall**
西安音乐厅 xī'ān yīnyuè tīng
Xi'an music hall

Public, Scenic Spaces

Figure 13.21 **Freedom square**

自由广场 zìyóu guǎngchǎng

This square in Taipei was renamed in 2007 from 大中至正门 which contains the characters 中 and 正, which constitute the alias of the former authoritarian ruler Chiang Kai-shek of ROC.

Figure 13.22 **National key scenic and famous site area**

国家重点风景名胜区 guójiā zhòngdiǎn fēngjǐng míngshèngqū

Figure 13.23 **Nine tribe culture village**

九族文化村 jiǔzú wénhuà cūn

This is a theme park in the scenic area of Sun Moon Lake (日月潭) featuring the cultures of the original inhabitants of Taiwan.

Figure 13.24 **Cable-car boarding point**

缆车搭乘处 lǎnchē dāchéng chù

搭 and 乘 can both mean 'to ride'.

大安森林公園
Daan Park

Figure 13.25 **Da'an forest park**
大安森林公园 dà'ān sēnlín gōngyuán
This is a park in Taipei, Taiwan.

北京中天行房车俱乐部
新疆喀纳斯房车营地

Figure 13.26 **Beijing Zhongtianxing RV club**
北京中天行房车俱乐部 běijīng zhōngtiānxíng fángchē jùlèbù
新疆喀纳斯房车营地 xīnjiāng kǎnàsī fángchē yíngdì
Xinjiang Kanasi RV campground
This is in the scenic area of Kanasi, Xinjiang. 俱乐部 is from English 'club'.

Miscellaneous

Figure 13.27 **Street artist**
台北县 táiběi xiàn | Taipei county
街头艺人 jiētóu yìrén | street artist
This is seen in the town 淡水, just north of Taipei.

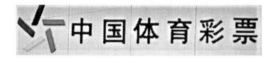

Figure 13.28 **China sports lotto**
中国体育彩票 zhōngguó tǐyù cǎipiào

Figure 13.29 **Free ticket**
赠票处 zèngpiào chù
赠 cannot be replaced with the synonymous 送,
which is spoken in style.

Figure 13.30 **Ticketing information**
购票须知 gòupiào xūzhī | buy ticket must know
购卡计费 gòukǎ jìfèi | buy card calculate charge
不予退换 bùyǔ tuìhuàn | not allow refund exchange
This is at a boat dock in Beihai Park in Beijing. 不予 is more formal than 不可
以. 须知 is from 必须知道.

Media

Figure 13.31 **TV channels**
本地 běndì | local
央视 yāngshì | CCTV
卫视 wèishì | satellite TV
广播 guǎngbō | radio
This is part of a TV channel lineup, with channels from cities and provinces. 央
视 is abbreviated from 中央电视台 'Chinese Central TV (CCTV)'. 卫视 is
abbreviated from 卫星电视 'satellite TV'.

Figure 13.32 **Traditional theatre**
戏曲 xìqǔ | theatrical tune
The word seems to be reserved for Chinese traditional opera.

Figure 13.33 **Super Hi-Def**

超高清 chāo gāoqīng | super high clear

高清 is the abbreviation for 高清晰度 'high clarity'.

Figure 13.34 **News night club**

新闻夜总会 xīnwén yèzǒnghuì

This was a feature of TVBS in Taiwan.

Figure 13.35 **Shanghai Radio**

上海电台 shànghǎi diàntái

Figure 13.36 **National education broadcast station**

国立教育广播电台 guólì jiàoyù guǎngbō diàntái

This is in Taipei, Taiwan.

Learning Outcomes

a. Gain familiarity with words related to cultural, scenic, and historical sites, entertainment venues, and media.

b. Gain some familiarity with artistic fonts.

Suggested Learning Activities

1. Using 博物, 纪念馆, 遗址, 故居, 故城, 旧址, search for names of museums and historical sites. Type them out and translate.
2. Using 庙and 寺, search for names of religious sites. Type them out and translate.
3. Using 影院, 剧院, 剧场, search for names of entertainment venues. Type them out and translate.
4. Using 公园 and 广场, search for names of parks and squares. Type them out and translate.
5. Using 频道 and 电台, search for names of TV channels and radio stations. Type them out and translate.
6. Using traditional characters, repeat the above searches for regions outside China.
7. Using the sign on boat rental (sign #30), select a boat and duration for your group and calculate the total cost.
8. Use words from this chapter in a narrative about a related topic (e.g. a weekend outing).

Alerts!

14

The signs in this chapter range from the strongest warnings to gentler reminders. 禁 (止) 'forbid' and 严禁 'strictly forbid' are used for the strongest warning possible. 请勿 'please don't' may be a tad less strong than 禁止. There are also other verbs of warning such as 莫 'don't', 不得 'must not' and 不可 'may not'. The most common reminders include verbs 当心 'beware of', 小心 'be careful about' and so on.

To convey a sense of seriousness, the language of warnings and reminders tends to be formal, replete with classical Chinese elements. For more examples of classical Chinese elements, see Chapter 2 on stylistic traits.

Figure 14.1 **Forbid/Please don't**
禁止摄影 jìnzhǐ shèyǐng | forbid photography
请勿踩踏 qǐngwù cǎità | please don't step on
禁止饮食 jìnzhǐ yǐnshí | forbid drinking eating
请勿触碰 qǐngwù chùpèng | please don't touch
This is seen in a museum in Shanghai.

| forbid inhale smoke
投诉电话 tóusù diànhuà | report phone
违者 wéizhě | violator
个人最高罚款 gèrén zuìgāo fákuǎn | individual highest penalty
场所最高罚款 chǎngsuǒ zuìgāo fákuǎn | venue highest penalty
上海市健康促进委员会 Shànghǎi shì jiànkāng cùjìn wěiyuánhuì
Shanghai health promotion commission

吸烟 is used instead of the spoken 抽烟 chōuyān 'draw smoke'. The classical 者 is used for the 'or' in 'violator'. The attention to smoking in public places has clearly increased, at least in the larger cities. This sign is rather more detailed than usual. The maximum fine for individuals is 200 RMB (about 30 USD) and maximum fine for venues is 30,000 (about 4,300 USD). Although the phone number 12345 to report violators sounds too simple to be real, online commentators have confirmed its validity.

Figure 14.3 **Strictly no smoking**
严禁吸烟 yánjìn xīyān
strict forbid inhale smoke
This is seen in Taiwan. 禁止 is shortened to 禁. 严 is added for emphasis.

Figure 14.4 **No smoking in toilet**
文明如厕 wénmíng rúcè | civilized use toilet
严禁吸烟 yánjìn xīyān | strict forbid inhale smoke
Be civilized in using toilet. Strictly forbid smoking.
There are two sentences here without any punctuation.
如厕 is a very fancy way of saying '上厕所'.

Figure 14.5 **No smoking in terminal**
航厦内全面禁烟 hángshà nèi quánmiàn jìnyān
aviation building inside complete forbid smoking
航厦 is used in Taiwan. 航站楼 is used in mainland.

Figure 14.6 **No selling tabaco and alcohol to minors**
禁止向未成年人出售烟酒商品
jìnzhǐ xiàng wèichéngniánrén chūshòu yānjiǔ shāngpǐn
forbid to not yet become person sell tobacco alcohol product
Selling tobacco and alcoholic products to minors is forbidden
未 in 未成年人 is classical for 没有. 出售 means the same as 售.

Figure 14.7 **No eating and drinking**
禁止饮食 jìnzhǐ yǐnshí | forbid drink eat
饮 and 食 are classical for 喝 and 吃 respectively.
They can no longer be used as verbs in speech in
modern Mandarin, though still used in Cantonese
this way.

Figure 14.8 **No playing**
禁止玩耍 jìnzhǐ wánshuǎ | forbid play
With the meaning of 玩, 耍 is more restricted in
usage. But it is used regularly in
southwestern Mandarin.

Figure 14.9 **No pushcart**
手推车禁止入内 shǒutuī chē jìnzhǐ rùnèi
hand push cart forbid enter in
入内 is classical for 进里边.

Figure 14.10 **No vehicle access**
禁止车辆通行 jìnzhǐ chēliàng tōngxíng
forbid vehicle through go
The 辆 in 车辆 is normally a measuring word
specifically for vehicles, but when it is used after
车, it makes the noun generic to refer to vehicles
in general rather than to specific ones. Similar
words are 纸张, 书本, and so on.

Figure 14.11 **No food from outside**
本店清真 běn diàn qīngzhēn | this store halal
外菜莫入 wàicài mòrù | outside dish no enter
禁止饮酒吸烟 jìnzhǐ yǐnjiǔ xīyān | forbid drink
谢谢合作 xièxie hézùo | thank cooperation
莫 is used instead of 别, as it goes better with

Figure 14.12 **No setting off firework**
外环线内禁止燃放烟花爆竹 wàihuánxiàn nèi jìnzhǐ ránfàng yānhuā bàozhú
outer ring line within forbid set off fireworks and firecrackers
洋泾街道平安办 yángjīng jiēdào píng'ānbàn | Yangjing street peace office
洋泾派出所 yángjīng pàichūsǔo | Yangjing police dispatch place
办 in 平安办 stands for 办公室. A 派出所 is like a police precinct in the United States.

Figure 14.13 **No firework unit**
禁放单位 jìn fàng dānwèi | forbid set off unit
禁放 is short for 禁止燃放. 单位 'unit' is Chinese
for workplace. There seem to be units such as
museums with cultural relics where firecrackers
are not allowed.

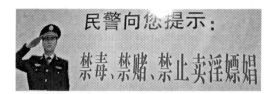

Figure 14.14 **No drugs, no gambling, no prostitution**
民警向您提示 mínjǐng xiàngnín tíshì | civil police to you remind
禁毒 jìndú | forbid drug
禁赌 jìndǔ | forbid gamble
禁止卖淫嫖娟 jìnzhǐ màiyín piáochāng | forbid prostitution
The choice between 禁止 and 禁 seems to depend on the number of resulting
syllables, with preference for even numbers. Also note the female radical in the
two characters for visiting a prostitute 嫖娟!

Please Don't!

Figure 14.15 **Please don't look at cellphone when riding escalators**
乘坐电梯时请勿看手机 chéngzuò diàntī shí qǐngwù kàn shǒujī
ride sit electric ladder time please not look hand machine
时 is 的时候 in spoken Chinese. 勿 is 别/不要 in spoken Chinese. The author
noted more than once that about half of the people riding escalators were looking
at their cellphones. Only the prospect of violating the rule prevented him from
taking a picture of it.

门灯闪烁 请勿上下车

Figure 14.16 **No going in and out of car when light is blinking**
门灯闪烁 méndēng shǎnshuò | door light blink
请勿上下车 qǐngwù shàngxiàchē | please don't go in out car

Figure 14.17 **Please don't play in water**
请勿戏水 qǐngwù xìshuǐ
Note the use of 戏 instead of 玩 for 'play'.

Figure 14.18 **Not going down on elevator**
注意 zhùyì | pay attention
电梯不可下行 diàntī bùkě xiàxíng
For this function, 不可 seems preferred than the longer 不可以.

Figure 14.19 **No exceeding load**
不得超载 bùdé chāozài
如校巴超载 rú xiàobā chāozài
if school bus exceed load
司机不准违法驾驶 sījī bùzhǔn wéifǎ jiàshǐ
driver not allow against law drive
不得 seems restricted to the formal style.

Figure 14.20 **Tourists stop**
游客止步 yóukè zhǐbù | tour guest stop step
Even though 止 means 停, for this function only
止步 can be used, and 停步 literally means
stopping steps.

Be Careful!

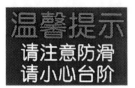

Figure 14.21 **Friendly reminder**
温馨提示 wēnxīn tíshì
请注意防滑 qǐng zhùyì fánghuá
please attention prevent slip
请小心台阶 qǐng xiǎoxīn táijiē | please careful steps

Figure 14.22 **Careful, floor is slippery**
小心地滑 xiǎoxīn dìhuá
small heart ground slippery

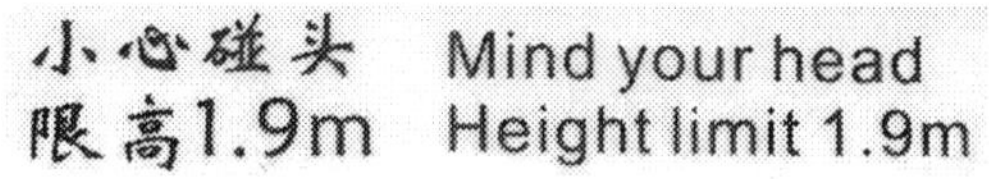

Figure 14.23 **Mind your head**
小心碰头 xiǎoxīn pèngtóu | small heart bump head
限高 xiàngāo | limit high

请小心保管
您的财物

Figure 14.24 **Please carefully take care**
请小心保管 qǐng xiǎoxīn bǎoguǎn
您的财物 nín de cáiwù | your valuable

Safety

Figure 14.25 **Safety exit**
安全出口 ānquán chūkǒu
peace whole out mouth

Figure 14.26 **Police**
警察 jǐngchá | vigilant observe (Police)
公安 gōngān | public peace (public security)
Public security bureau is 公安局.

Figure 14.27 **Security booth**
治安亭 zhì'ān tíng | manage peace booth

Figure 14.28 **Close door behind you, prevent being tailed**
随手关门 suíshǒu guānmén | follow hand close door
谨防尾随 jǐnfáng wěisuí | cautious prevent tail follow

Figure 14.29 **Video surveillance**
您已进入24小时监控区域 nín yǐ jìnrù 24 xiǎoshí jiānkòng qūyù
you already enter 24 hour monitor control zone
已 is preferred over the full form 已经. 进入 is a mixed compound, with modern
进 and classical 入, both meaning 'enter'.

Figure 14.30 **Dropping off and loading only**
临时上下客 línshí shàngxià kè
temporary up down guest

Figure 14.31 **Be careful, fire hazard**
当心火灾 dāngxīn huǒzāi
careful fire disaster

Figure 14.32 **Fire hydrant**

消火栓 xiāohuǒ shuān | extinguish fire hydrant

灭火器 mièhuǒ qì | extinguish fire device

火警 huǒjǐng | fire warning

消 and 灭 both mean 'extinguish'. They can even form a compound 消灭, which means to 'wipe out (enemy)'. But the choice between 消 and 灭 seems fixed. While 消火器 is occasionally seen, *灭火栓 does not seem to exit.

Figure 14.33 **Xiushui building fire escape route map**

秀水大厦逃生疏散图 xiùshuǐ dàshà táoshēng shūsàn tú

xiushui big building escape life disperse chart

Learning Outcomes

a. Gain familiarity with warning and reminder signs.
b. Gain familiarity with key common elements in warning and reminder signs.
c. Gain greater awareness of the use of written-style words in public signs.

Suggested Learning Activities

1. Using 禁止, 严禁, 禁, 请勿, 不得, 不可, 止步, 小心, and 当心, search for signs online. Type them out and translate.
2. Using traditional characters, repeat the above searches for regions outside China.
3. Identify written-style elements in found signs.
4. Paraphrase written-style signs in spoken style.
5. Analyze mistranslations in bilingual signs and correct them.
6. What is the most forceful way to say 'not allowed'? What is the least?
7. Use 禁止, 严禁, 禁, 请勿, 不得, 不可, 止步, 小心, and 当心 to create signs.

Health   15

This chapter includes several public announcements from past pandemics, images of medicine, medical care, and various offices and departments in a neighborhood community clinic in Shanghai.

Figure 15.1 **First aid**
医疗急救 yīliáo jíjiù
medical urgent rescue

Pandemic-related

The signs below were collected before the COVID pandemic. But they are as applicable today as back then.

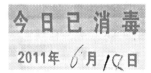

Figure 15.2 **Today already disinfected**
今日已消毒 jīnrì yǐ xiāodú
2011年6月18日 | 2011 year 6 month 18 day
今日 is used instead of 今天, 已 instead of 已经. This was seen after the H1N1 pandemic in 2009.

Figure 15.3 **This hall is thoroughly disinfected**
本大厅 běn dàtīng | this hall
已全面消毒 yǐ quánmiàn xiāodú | already all side disinfect
请安心使用 qǐng ānxīn shǐyòng | please peace of mind use
This was seen in Taiwan.

Figure 15.4 **All people guard against H1N1**
全民防范 H1N1 quánmín fángfàn H1N1
勤洗手 qín xǐshǒu | frequently wash hands
保健康 bǎo jiànkāng | protect health
This was seen in Taiwan.

Figure 15.5 **Prevent flu**
预防流感 yùfáng liúgǎn
进入馆舍请使用 jìnrù guǎnshě qǐng shǐyòng
enter building please use
干性洗手剂 gānxìng xǐshǒu jì
dry wash hand agent
This was posted in a university library in Taiwan.

Figure 15.6 **Treasure life**
珍惜生命 zhēnxī shēngmìng
让艾远离 ràng ài yuǎnlí | let AIDS be far
艾滋病的传播途径 àizībìng de chuánbō tújìng | AIDS disease spread channel
The ad hoc abbreviation 艾 is incomprehensible without the accompanying full
version 艾滋病. The abbreviation reduces the syllable count to four, to be
parallel with the phrase above it. Interestingly, 艾 sounds like 爱 'love' and 爱滋
is another word for AIDS. 珍惜…远离 is a common pattern.

Figure 15.7 **Seek 1,000 people**
寻找1000名 xúnzhǎo 1000 míng
慢病患者 mànbìng huànzhě | slow illness patient
糖尿病 tángniàobìng | diabetes
高血压 gāo xuěyā | hypertension
高血脂 gāo xuězhī | hyperlipidemia
This is an ad looking for participants for a clinical trial. A mixed compound 寻
(classical) 找(non-classical) is used for 'seek'.

Figure 15.8 **Dentist**
晶致牙医 jīngzhì yáyī | crystal ultimate dental doctor
There may be an attempt at puns. 晶 can suggest 'sparkling'; 晶致 sounds the
same as 精致, which means meticulous.

Figure 15.9 **Ophthalmologist Chen**
陈眼科 chén yǎnkē | Chen eye department
耳鼻喉科 ěrbíhóu kē | ear nose throat department
This is seen in Taiwan. Note the vertical, right-to-left format.

Figure 15.10 **Siam palace Thai style wellness center**
暹罗宫泰式养生馆 xiānluó gōng tàishì yǎngshēng guǎn
预约专线yùyuē zhuānxiàn | reservation special line

Drugstore and Drug

Figure 15.11 **Health pharmacy**
健康药房 jiànkāng yàofáng
health medicine house

Figure 15.12 **Drugstore**
药店 yàodiàn | medicine store
This chain drugstore is in Boston's Chinatown.

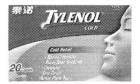

Figure 15.13 **Tylenol**
泰诺 tàinuò
Although this is obviously based on transliteration, the character 泰 does mean 'peace'. Both 泰 and 诺, along with 康 and 宁, are frequently used in names of medicines.

A Hospital and a Clinic in Shanghai

Figure 15.14 **Xuhui district central hospital**
徐汇区中心医院
xúhuìqū zhōngxīn yīyuàn
The name of this hospital in Shanghai is written in the vertical format and traditional characters.

Figure 15.15 **Yangjing community health service center**
洋泾社区卫生服务中心
yángjīng shèqū wèishēng fúwù zhōngxīn
Community clinics like this one are found throughout Chinese cities. They are different from full-scale hospitals in having no in-patient services.

Figure 15.16 **Registration/Cashier**
挂号 guàhào | hang number
收费 shōufèi | collect fee

Figure 15.17 **Infusion/injection room**
输液室 shūyè shì | input liquid room
注射室 zhùshè shì | injection room
What is translated as 'transfusion' is for IV injection.

Figure 15.18 **Radiology**
放射科 fàngshè kē
radiology department
B stands for basement.
科 'department' is the basic unit in a hospital.

Figure 15.19 **First floor**
挂号收费 guàhào shōufèi | registration and cashier
放射科医生办公室 fàngshè kē yīsheng bàngōngshì | radiology doctor office
全科诊室 quánkē zhěnshì | general practice room
眼科 yǎnkē | ophthalmology department
皮肤科 pífū kē | dermatology department
家床办公室 jiāchuáng bàngōngshì | home bed office
医患沟通室 yīhuàn gōutōng shì | doctor-patient communication room
输液室 shūyè shì | transfusion room
化验室 huàyàn shì | lab room
西药房 xīyàofáng | western medicine pharmacy
医患 'doctor-patient' is abbreviated from 医生 and 患者.

Figure 15.20 **Second floor**
收费 shōufèi | cashier
中医内科 zhōngyī nèikē | Chinese internal medicine
中医推拿 zhōngyī tuīná | Chinese massage medicine
中医伤科 zhōngyī shāng kē | Chinese traumatology medicine
中医治未病 zhōngyī zhìwèibìng | Chinese preventive medicine
中药房 zhōng yàofáng | Chinese medicine pharmacy
康复治疗室 kāngfù zhìliáo shì | rehabilitation therapy room
口腔科 kǒuqiāng kē | oral medicine department
妇女保健室 fùnǚ bǎojiàn shì | women wellness room
妇科 fùkē | gynecology department
计划生育指导室 jìhuà shēngyù zhǐdǎo shì | plan birth guidance room
更年期咨询室 gēngniánqī zīxún shì | menopause consultation room

Figure 15.21 **Third floor**
哮喘门诊 xiàochuǎn ménzhěn | asthma consultation
B超室 B chāo shì | ultrasound room
心电图室 xīndiàntú shì | electrocardiogram room
信息科 xìnxī kē | information department
中医针灸 zhōngyī zhēnjiǔ | Chinese acupuncture
会议室 huìyì shì | conference room
全科团队工作室 quánkē tuánduì gōngzuò | general teamwork room
超in B 超 is short for 超声波 'ultra sound wave'. B stands for brightness. The bi-script abbreviation is quite unusual!

Figure 15.22 **Fourth floor**
医务科 yīwù kē | medical department
预防保健科 yùfáng bǎojiàn kē | preventive health care department
护理部 hùlǐ bù | nursing department
院感办公室 yuàngǎn bàngōngshì | hospital infection office
全科团队服务科 quánkē tuánduì fúwù kē | general practice team service department
工会 gōnghuì | union
会议室 huìyì shì | conference room
院感 'hospital infection' is abbreviated from 医院感染.

Figure 15.23 **Fifth floor**

主任室 zhǔrèn shì | director's office
书记室 shūjì shì | (party) secretary's office
副主任室 fù zhǔrèn shì | deputy director's office
综合办公室 zōnghé bàngōngshì | general office
人事科 rénshì kē | personnel department
财务科 cáiwù kē | financial department
后勤保障科 hòuqín bǎozhàng kē | logistic support department
安全办 ānquán bàn | security office
The 办 in 安全办 is abbreviated from 办公室. Note that top administration occupies the top floor!

Learning Outcomes

a. Gain familiarity with terms related to health and medicine.
b. Gain familiarity with different departments of hospitals and clinics.
c. Gain greater awareness of the use of abbreviations.

Suggested Learning Activities

1. Using 医院, 门诊, 诊所, 牙医, 口腔科, and 卫生所, search online for related signs.
2. Using traditional characters to search for signs from regions outside of China.
3. Identify abbreviations and find out what the full terms are.
4. What do 科 and 室 mean? Find all the 科s and 室s in this chapter and Chapter 12 and translate them.
5. Using Google Translate, translate some Western drugs into Chinese. Which characters are used most often?
6. Use signs relating to hospital in a narrative on a related topic (e.g. seeing the doctor).

Part III
Other Signs

16   Advertising

The ads sampled in this chapter are of three types: commercials, classified ads, and the so-called small ads.

Commercials

Commercials can appeal to senses of good value, tradition and authenticity, novelty and popularity. To attract attention, they often employ
rhetorical devices such as punning, parallelism, allusions to shared
cultural knowledge, and unexpected juxtaposition for humorous effect.
For more examples of punning and parallelism, see Chapter 3.

Formal Appeal

Figure 16.1 **Heart of cognac**
心中干邑 xīnzhōng gānyì | heart mid cognac
干邑中心 gānyì zhōngxīn | cognac mid heart
This ad plays on the reversal of 心中 'in heart' and 中心 'center'. The two parts
look like mirror images but for 干邑, and still manage to make sense.

Figure 16.2 **Wanda**
万达所至 wàndá suǒ zhì | Wanda arrive
中心所在 zhōngxīn suǒ zài | center be
(Wherever Wanda goes, that's where the center will be.)
This ad employs formal symmetry, with four characters in each line and 所__ in
both lines. 所 is a classical particle. 至 is classical for 到. The Wanda Group is a
major multinational conglomerate.

Figure 16.3 **I choose my taste**
我选我味 wǒ xuǎn wǒ wèi
This is a fast-food ad. Both Chinese and English are four syllables long, broken into two disyllabic parts. 我 is shared by both lines. The symmetry lies between Chinese and English, as well as within Chinese.

Unexpected Twists

Figure 16.4 **Quit smoke quit alcohol quit lover**
戒烟戒酒戒情人 jièyān jièjiǔ jiè qíngrén
Quitting lover!

Figure 16.5 **Add alcohol station**
加酒站 jiājiǔ zhàn
This is from 加油站 'gas station'. 酒 and 油 also rhyme.

Figure 16.6 **Luzhi drink alcohol training base**
用直喝酒培训基地 lùzhí hējiǔ péixùn jīdì
欢迎光临 huānyíng guānglín | welcome presence
可以喝酒 kěyǐ hējiǔ | can drink alcohol
可以发呆 kěyǐ fādāi | can stare into space
可以蹭网 kěyǐ cèngwǎng | can freeload on Wi-Fi
We are so accustomed to 不可以 'not allowed'!

Figure 16.7 **This place forbids talking price**
此地禁止讲价 cǐdì jìnzhǐ jiǎngjià
This is at a bazaar. Not to bargain here is almost a crime! 此地 is classical for 这个地方. Traditional characters are used even though it is in mainland China.

Allusions

Ads with these may be baffling to outsiders, as they attempt to appeal to shared cultural knowledge.

Figure 16.8 **Friendly guest appearance**
友情客串 yǒuqíng kèchuàn
The allusion is to cameo appearance in movie making. 串 'skewer' is a favorite street food.

Figure 16.9 **Happy little lamb**
快乐小羊 kuàilè xiǎoyáng
One can hardly avoid the association with one of the most famous hotpot chains 小肥羊 'little fat lamb'.

Figure 16.10 **Helen Keller**
海伦凯勒 hǎilún kǎillè
眼镜 yǎnjìng | eyeglasses
Whether or not it is advisable, the allusion to
the inspirational blind author is unmistakable.

Old, Homey, and Authentic!

Figure 16.11 **Old Shanghai scallion oil pancake**
老上海葱油饼 lǎo shànghǎi cōngyóu bǐng
顾寿刚 gù shòugāng | Shougang Gu
创始于 1983 chuàngshǐ yú | founded in 1983
This is the oil-stained wrapper of a local favorite.
于 is classical Chinese for 'in'.

Figure 16.12 **Ceremoniously push out (introduce)**
隆重推出 lóngzhòng tuīchū
纯手工老面包子 chún shǒugōng lǎomiàn bāozi
pure hand work old dough steamed bun
让你找到小时候的味道
ràngnǐ zhǎodào xiǎoshíhoude wèidào
let you find small time (childhood) flavor

Figure 16.13 **Hunan west grandma vegetable rice**
湘西外婆菜饭 xiāngxī wàipó càifàn
This tries to appeal to nostalgia for family
and hometown.

Figure 16.14 **Authentic Japanese food**
甘醇味美 gānchún wèiměi | sweet delicious
正宗日本料理 zhèngzōng rìběn liàolǐ
authentic Japanese cooking
Part of the authenticity is in the use of 料理, the Japanese word for cooking.

New and Popular!

Figure 16.15 **Popular new product**
人气新品 rénqì xīnpǐn
酸汤莜面鱼鱼 suāntāng yóumiàn yúyu
sour soup oat fish fish (spaetzle)
蘑菇汤莜面鱼鱼 mógūtāng yóumiàn yúyu
mushroom soup oat fish fish (spaetzle)
人气 'popular' is from Japanese 人気 (ninki).

Figure 16.16 **Sales champion**
销量冠军 xiāoliàng guànjūn
辣黄牛炒莜面 là huángniú chǎo yóumiàn
spicy yellow cow stir-fry oat noodle
葱油虾仁拌莜面 cōngyóu xiārén bàn yóumiàn
scallion oil shrimp mix oat noodle

Free and Cheap!

Figure 16.17 **Non-alcoholic drink**
非酒精饮品 fēi jiǔjīng yǐnpǐn
免费续杯 miǎnfèi xùbēi | no fee continue cup (free refill)
(限同款) xiàn tóngkuǎn | limit to same style
The operative word is 免费 'free'!

Figure 16.18 **Super value**
一杯咖啡的价格 yìbēi kāfēi de jiàgé
a cup coffee price
在这里搞定一套 zài zhèlǐ gǎodìng yítào
here get a set
货真价实好超值 hùozhēnjiàshí hǎo chāozhí
stuff real price solid so super value
'Great value' is conveyed by both 货真价实
and 超值.

Safe to Eat!

When restaurants resort to ads like these, there must be cause
for concern!

Figure 16.19 **Cow sheep meat**
牛羊肉 niúyángròu
安全放心 ānquán fàngxīn | safe, be at ease

Figure 16.20 **Our promise**
我们de承诺 wǒmen de chéngnuò
面食不用洗衣粉 miànshí búyòng xǐyīfěn
wheat food not use wash clothes powder
调料不用防腐剂 tiáoliào búyòng fángfǔjì
seasoning not use preservative
做饭不用病死肉 zuòfàn búyòng bìngsǐ ròu
make food not use sick dead meat
炒菜不用地沟油 chǎocài búyòng dìgōu yóu
stir-fry not use earth ditch (recycled) oil
Amazingly, the disturbing message is conveyed through neat formal symmetry,
which includes the consistent use of the topic-comment structure (topic=as for).

Job Ads: These Restaurants Are Hiring

Figure 16.21 **Hiring**

招聘 zhāopìn | recruit hire

服务员 fúwù yuán | server

厨房工 chúfáng gōng | kitchen worker

勤杂工 qínzá gōng | misc. worker (handy person)

名 míng | measure for people

包吃包住 bāochī bāozhù | include food include lodging

工资待遇面议 gōngzī dàiyù miànyì | salary treatment face talk

面议 'discuss face-to-face' is a formulaic expression.

Figure 16.22 **Hiring**

招聘 zhāopìn | recruit hire

凉菜师 liángcài shī | cold dish master

墩子 dūnzi | cutting board (prep cook)

工资面议 gōngzī miànyì | salary face talk

服务员 fúwùyuán | server

工资 gōngzī | salary

奖金 jiǎngjīn | award gold (bonus)

开瓶费 kāipíng fèi | open bottle fee (corkage)

男女不限 nánnǚ búxiàn | male female no restriction

Figure 16.23 **Hiring**
掌柜小店 zhǎngguì xiǎodiàn
shopkeeper little shop
掌柜招聘 zhǎngguì zhāopìn
shopkeeper recruit hire
招聘岗位 zhāopìn gǎngwèi
recruit hire position
店长 diànzhǎng | general manager
主管 zhǔguǎn | kitchen manager
服务员 fúwùyuán | server
厨工 chúgōng | kitchen worker
Note the old-style word 掌柜 'proprietor'.

Classified Ads

Classified ads can be seen in newspapers or message boards at super-
markets. They are noteworthy for having a cryptic style, being short, and
being full of abbreviations and formulaic expressions, sometimes without punctuation marks.

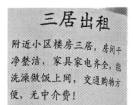

Figure 16.24 **For rent**
三居出租 sān jū chūzū | 3 room out rent
附近小区楼房三居 fùjìn xiǎoqū lóufáng sānjū
nearby sub-division building 3 room
房间干净整洁 fángjiān gānjìng zhěngjié | rooms clean tidy
家具家电齐全 jiājù jiādiàn qíquán | furniture home appliance complete
能洗澡做饭上网 néng xǐzǎo zuòfàn shàngwǎng | can take bath cook go online
交通购物方便 jiāotōng gòuwù fāngbiàn | transportation shopping convenient
无中介费 wú zhōngjiè fèi | no middle introduction (broker) fee
三居 and 家电 are abbreviations for 三个居室 and 家用电器 respectively.

Help Wanted
请全职/兼职前台一位
有意者请电

Figure 16.25 **Hiring receptionist**
请全职/兼职前台一位 qǐng quánzhí/jiānzhí qiántái yíwèi
hire full time/part time receptionist 1 person
有意者请电 yǒuyìzhě qǐngdiǎn | interested person please call
(有)意者请电 is formulaic, meaning 有兴趣的人请打电话.

Figure 16.26 **Restaurant hiring**
餐馆诚征 cānguǎn chéngzhēng
restaurant earnest seek
诚征前台 chéngzhēng qiántái | earnest seek front desk
服务生/帮厨 fúwùshēng/bāngchú |server/kitchen help
和外送人员 hé wàisòng rényuán | and delivery person
诚征 is a formulaic expression. El Cajon is in San Diego.

Small Ads

Small ads 小广告 are so called because they are extremely short, with just the name of the service and the phone number. Very informal, some are handwritten. They are put up in elevators, on lamp posts, anywhere people may see them, obviously without seeking permission or paying for them. They have become somewhat of a nuisance.

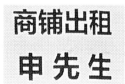

Figure 16.27 **Store for rent**
商铺出租 shāngpù chūzū
commercial store for rent
申先生 shēn xiānsheng
Mr. Shen

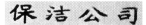

Figure 16.28 **Cleaning**
保洁 bǎojié | cleaning
公司 gōngsī | company

Figure 16.29 **Unclog drain**
专通下水道 zhuān tōng xiàshuǐdào
specialty unclog drain
管道清洗 guǎndào qīngxǐ
pipe/duct cleaning

Figure 16.30 **Certificate and seal**
办证 bànzhèng | do certificate
刻章 kèzhāng | carve seal
The ethics of 办证 seems questionable.

Figure 16.31 **Provide egg surrogate pregnancy**
供卵代孕 gōngluǎn dàiyùn
包生男孩 bāoshēng nánhái
guarantee birth male child
The guarantee is questionable.

Learning Outcomes

a. Gain familiarity with different kinds of ads.
b. Gain familiarity with different strategies used in ads for goods.
c. Gain familiarity with formulaic expressions used in classified ads.

Suggested Learning Activities

1. How many strategies are used in product/food ads in this chapter?
2. Using 诚征 and 招聘, search online for job ads. Type them out and translate.
3. Using 出租 and (有)意者请电, search online for rental ads. Type them out and translate.
4. Using 小广告, search online for small ads. Type them out and translate.
5. Using traditional characters, repeat the above searches for other regions.

6. Identify classical Chinese elements and abbreviations in found ads.
7. Identify formulaic expressions in found classified ads.
8. Identify punning and parallelism in product/food ads.
9. Design an ad for a product/food. What strategies listed in this chapter will you use?
10. Write a classified ad. Use 有意者请电 and abbreviations if necessary.
11. Write a small ad.

Civic Signs

Civic signs and political banners seem to be particularly numerous in China. They are used to extol civic and cultural values reflecting the current social and political climate. From their contents, one can get a sense of what are considered important at a particular time.

Like couplets, the rhetorical device of parallelism is frequently employed.

Conserve!

Figure 17.1 **Please save water**
请节约用水 qǐng jiéyuē yòngshuǐ
Please save use water

Figure 17.2 **Be frugal**
人人节约 rénrén jiéyuē | person person (everyone) frugal
家家有余 jiājiā yǒuyú | household household (every household) have surplus
福 fú | blessing
Both punning and parallelism are used. 余 is homophonous with 鱼 'fish', which explains the image of fish. More often though, 鱼 is used to suggest 余 'surplus'. The first two characters of both four-character lines are repeated.

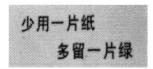

Figure 17.3 **Save paper**

少用一片纸 shǎoyòng yípiàn zhǐ | less use one piece paper
多留一片绿 duōliú yípiàn lǜ | more leave one piece green
Note the ample use of parallelism and contrast in this short sign. 片 in the
second line is used metaphorically, meaning an expanse of green.

Figure 17.4 **Scan code to get toilet paper**

扫码取纸 sǎomǎ qǔzhǐ | scan code take paper
环保新方式 huánbǎo xīn fāngshì
environment protection new way
环保 is abbreviated from 环境保护.

Sort That Trash!

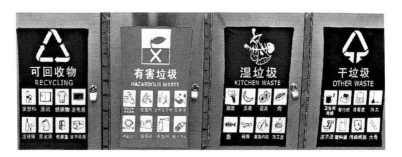

Figure 17.5 **Types of trash**

可回收物	有害垃圾	湿垃圾	干垃圾
kě huíshōu wù	yǒuhài lājī	shī lājī	gān lājī
recyclable stuff	harmful trash	wet trash	dry trash

Note 垃圾 is pronounced lèsè in Taiwan.

Figure 17.6 **Don't go to wrong door**
不要走错门 búyào zǒucuò mén
not want go wrong door
垃圾也有家 lājī yěyǒu jiā
trash also has home

Figure 17.7 **Sort trash green life**
生活垃圾分一分 shēnghuó lājī fēn yì fēn | life trash divide a bit
绿色生活一百分 lǜsè shēnghuó yì bǎi fēn | green life 100 point
联洋社区 liányáng shèqū | Lianyang community
宣 xuān | announce
Both lines can be divided into a four-character and a three-character part.
Both lines contain 生活; both end with 分, ensuring rhyming of the lines.

Be Civilized!

Figure 17.8 **Be civilized and courteous**
文明礼让 wénmíng lǐràng
civilized ritual yield

Figure 17.9 **Create civilized town**
创全国文明城 chuàng quánguó wénmíng chéng
create (in) whole country civilized town
做黄埔文明人 zuò huángpǔ wénmíng rén
be Huangpu civilized person
The line on the right is read first. Both lines follow the pattern: verb + place + civilized + noun. Huangpu is a district in Shanghai by the river of the same name.

Figure 17.10 **Promote clean governing culture**
弘扬廉政文化 hóngyáng liánzhèng wénhuà
共建和谐文明 gòngjiàn héxié wénmíng
together build harmony civilization
In addition to the similarity between the last words of each line 文化/文明, parallelism is also in the shared pattern for the lines: verb+modifier+noun.

Figure 17.11 **Civilization come from one bit one drop**
文明来自一点一滴 wénmíng láizì yìdiǎn yìdī
新风源起一言一行 xīnfēng yuánqǐ yìyán yìxíng
new atmosphere source from one word one deed
Note the parallelism and contrast between the two lines.

Figure 17.12 **Lean closer to civilization**
贴近方便 tiējìn fāngbiàn | lean close convenience
靠近文明 kàojìn wénmíng | lean close civilization
Unlikely juxtaposition of parallelism and the mundane context. 方便 is a
euphemism for urinate.

Stay Away from Committing Crime!

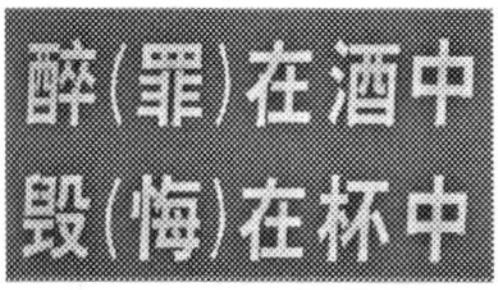

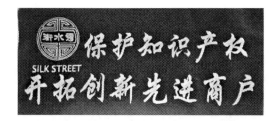

Figure 17.13 **Don't drink and drive**
醉(罪)在酒中 zuì zài jiǔzhōng | drunk (crime) in alcohol
毁(悔)在杯中 huǐ zài bēizhōng | ruin (regret) in cup
醉 'drunk' and 罪 'crime' are homophonous, as are 毁 'ruin' and 悔 'regret'. But
the puns are spoiled! Note the close parallelism.

Figure 17.14 **Protect intellectual property right**
保护知识产权 bǎohù zhīshi chǎnquán
开拓创新先进商户 kāituò chuàngxīn xiānjìn shānghù
develop innovative progressive business
Ironically, this is seen in 秀水街 in Beijing, known for its counterfeit goods.

Be Courteous

Figure 17.15 **Line up**
请在此排队
qǐng zàicǐ páiduì
please at here line up
此 is classical for 这儿 'here'.

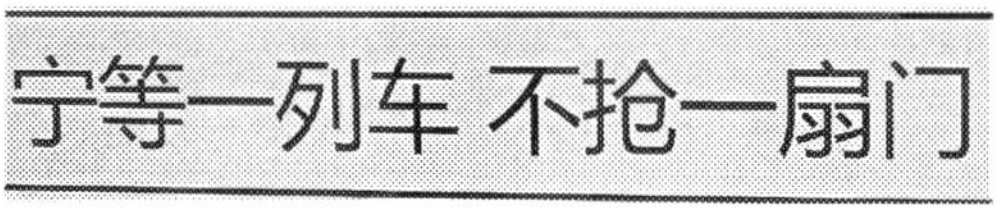

宁等一列车 不抢一扇门

Figure 17.16 **Be patient**
宁等一列车 níng děng yíliè chē | rather wait a car
不抢一扇门 bù qiǎng yíshàn mén | not crash one door
This is on doors of subway trains. Points of parallelism and contrast: 宁vs.不 (adverb); 等vs. 抢 (verb); 列 vs. 扇 (measure); 车 vs. 门 (noun).

Figure 17.17 **Buy ticket**
有我高 yǒu wǒ gāo | have I tall
(If you are as tall as I am)
请买票 qǐng mǎipiào | please buy ticket
Parallelism and contrast can still be seen in such a short sign. Both 有我 and 请买 are third-tone sequences with tone change. 高 and 票 rhyme but provide tonal variation.

Figure 17.18 **Light sound quiet word I like**
轻声细语我喜欢 qīngshēngxìyǔ wǒ xǐhuān
地铁行 dìtiě xíng | subway travel
文明行 wénmíng xíng | civilized travel

Figure 17.19 **No dirty words**
不说粗话脏话 bù shuō cūhuà zānghuà
not speak coarse word dirty word
杭州市文明办宣 hángzhōu shì wénmíngbàn xuān
Hangzhou city civilization office announce
办 in 文明办 is abbreviated from 办公室.

Figure 17.20 **Civilized dining table action**
文明餐桌行动 wénmíng cānzhuō xíngdòng
不剩菜 bú shèngcài | not leave food
不劝酒 bú quànjiǔ | not persuade to drink alcohol
不吸烟 bù xīyān | not inhale smoke
That there is need for such a reminder means that
these behaviors are very common!

Core Civic Values

Figure 17.21 **Honesty**
国无诚信不强 guó wú chéngxìn bù qiáng
country not trustworthy not strong
业无诚信不兴 yè wú chéngxìn bù xīng
business not trustworthy not flourish
人无诚信不立 rén wú chéngxìn bú lì
person not trustworthy not established
The parallelism is extreme. The three lines share
four out of six characters: 无诚信不.

.22 **Core values**

义核心价值观 shèhuìzhǔyì héxīn jiàzhíguān | socialist core value view

信仰 rénmín yǒu xìnyǎng | people have faith 国家有力量 guójiā yǒu lìliàng | country have strength

uójiā | country

qiáng | wealthy 民主 mínzhǔ | democratic 文明 wénmíng | civilized 和谐 héxié | harmonious

ɪèhuì | society

yóu | free 平等 píngděng | equal 公正 gōngzhèng | just 法制 fǎzhì | rule by law

rén | individual

guó | patriotic 敬业 jìngyè dedicated | 诚信 chéngxìn | trustworthy 友善 yǒushàn | friendly

Political Banners

Figure 17.23 **Not forget first heart**
不忘初心 búwàng chūxīn
为人民谋幸福 wèi rénmín móu xìngfú | for people seek happiness
牢记使命 láojì shǐmìng | firm remember mission
为民族谋复兴 wèi mínzú móu fùxīng | for nation seek revival
–加强未成年人思想道德建设 | jiāqiáng wèichéngniánrén sīxiǎng dàodé jiànshè
strengthen adolescent thought and moral building
关爱未成年人健康成长 guān'ài wèichéngniánrén jiànkāng chéngzhǎng
attention love adolescent healthy growth
The first two lines have 4+6 characters each, with points of similarity and contrast.
The last two longer lines though are not quite perfectly symmetrical.

Figure 17.24 **Strike black banish evil**

保持高压态势 bǎochí gāoyā tàishì | maintain high pressure momentum

铁腕打黑除恶 tiěwàn dǎhēi chú'è | iron wrist strike black rid evil

人民安居乐业 rénmín ānjūlèyè | people live in peace and work in happiness

社会安定有序 shèhuì āndìng yǒuxù | society peaceful orderly

国家长治久安 guójiā chángzhìjiǔ'ān | country long-term stability

严打黑恶犯罪 yándǎ hēi è fànzuì | severe strike black evil and crime

弘扬社会正气 hóngyáng shèhuì zhèngqì | promote social justice

This is seen in the small water town 甪直 lùzhí near Suzhou. All lines are six characters long. Quite unusually, there is no attempt at rhyming.

Learning Outcomes

a. Gain awareness of the relationship between public signs and society.

b. Gain awareness of the relationship between signs and changing political climate.

c. Gain greater awareness of the use of parallelism in public signs.

Suggested Learning Activities

1. Using 节约, 环保, and 文明, search online for signs containing these words. Type them out and translate.

2. Identify punning and parallelism in the found signs.

3. Using the 历时检索 function from the BCC corpus (http://bcc.blcu .edu.cn/hc), find out when 打黑, 不忘初心 and核心价值 started to be used.

4. Using words from this chapter, design a civic sign.

18 Dialectal Elements

Reflecting the cultural and regional diversity in China, signs may contain dialectal elements, especially those of the major dialects such as Cantonese, Min, and Shanghai/Wu.

Dialects can differ in vocabulary and grammar, and particularly in sound. The differences in sound can sometimes be seen in phonetic transliterations. Dialectal words are those that do not have counterparts in the standard language. They are often written by borrowing standard characters just for the sound without regard to their original meaning (Rebus Principle); they can also be written in specially created dialectal characters.

Dialects can also resemble classical Chinese, as they tend to retain features of older Chinese.

As dialectal influence is widely seen in the Chinese diaspora, more examples of dialectal elements can be seen in Chapter 19.

Cantonese

Among all Chinese dialects, Cantonese enjoys a special status, as it is spoken in Guangdong, Hong Kong, Macau, and diaspora communities all over the world.

Pronunciation Difference

Note that pronunciation is given in Mandarin, as romanization for Cantonese is not as standardized and may not be familiar to readers.

Figure 18.1 **Zhou big blessing**
周大福 zhōu dà fú
This is a jewelry chain from Hong Kong. Its Cantonese origin is reflected in the transliteration, which has the final 'k' in Fook. The other two final consonants are 'p' and 't'.

興盛糕點
HING SHING PASTRY

Figure 18.2 **Prosperous pastry**
兴盛糕点 xīngshèng gāodiǎn
Hing Shing is how Cantonese pronounces 兴盛. This is in Boston's Chinatown.

HEYTEA 喜茶

Figure 18.3 **Like tea**
喜茶 xǐ chá
In Cantonese, 喜 is pronounced like 'hey' in English.

Vocabulary Difference

請行入車廂
Please move in

Figure 18.4 **Please walk into compartment**
请行入车厢 qǐng xíngrù chēxiāng
The classical 行 and 入 cannot be used this way in Mandarin; they can only be
used in compounds such as 行人 'pedestrian' and 入口 'entrance'.

LOWER DECK SEATING 樓下座位 28
STANDING 樓下企位 41

Figure 18.5 **Downstairs standing**
楼下座位 lóuxià zuòwèi | downstairs seating
楼下企位 lóuxià qǐwèi | downstairs standing
This is on a double-decker bus in Hong Kong. 企 is Cantonese for 'to stand'.
In Mandarin it is used in the word 企鹅 'penguin', which means standing goose!

Figure 18.6 **Cooked dish**
熟餸 shú sòng
外卖 wàimài | out sell
餸 is a bona fide Cantonese word. This is seen in
San Francisco's Chinatown, where the common
language is Cantonese.

Figure 18.7 **For food specialist**
为食家 wèishí jiā | gourmand/glutton
为食 is Cantonese for 'greedy for food'.
This restaurant is in Boston's Chinatown.

Cantonese Words with Rare or Borrowed Characters

Figure 18.8 **Drop ship take Hong Kong rail**
落船搭港铁 luòchuán dā gǎngtiě
即悭$1.5 jí qiān $1.5 | instant save $1.5
(Take Hong Kong rail after disembarking from ship, save $1.5 right away.)
The rare word 悭 'to save' is still used in speech in Cantonese. 落 is Cantonese for 下, 搭 for 乘 'ride'.

Figure 18.9 **Eaten yet?**
食左未 shí zuǒ wèi | eat particle not (eaten yet)
吃了没 chī le méi | eat particle not (eaten yet)
The Cantonese version in big characters is glossed with small characters in Mandarin. 食 and 未 are Cantonese (also classical Chinese) for 吃 and 没 respectively. 左 'left' is borrowed to write the sound of the perfective particle 'tso' in Cantonese.

Figure 18.10 **Bull**
牛 niú | bull 就係我嘅態度 jiùxì wǒkǎi tàidù | just my attitude
This was seen in a beef ball soup restaurant. The big character 牛 is a pun, as it can also mean 'arrogantly awesome'. The line below reinforces the pun. 係 (=是) and 嘅 (=的) are created to write the dialect words.

Figure 18.11 **Walk a bit faster**
行快D啦 喂 | xíng kuài D la wèi
全场七折 | quánchǎng qīzhé
D is used in place of the identical sounding 啲, a Cantonese character created by adding 口 to show that it is used phonetically. 行 is Cantonese (and classical Chinese) for 走 'walk'.

Shanghai/Wu

The Wu dialect, with its most populous metropolis Shanghai, is one of the major dialect families of China.

Figure 18.12 **Shanghai people**
上海宁 shànghǎi níng
老玩具有伐 lǎo wánjù yǒu fá | old toy have question particle
This ad is from McDonald's. The use of 宁 illustrates the Rebus Principle. 宁 'peace', not at all related in meaning to 人 'person', is used for its sound only. The same is true with writing the question particle with 伐, which otherwise means 'chopping down trees'.

Figure 18.13 **I/we Ningbo**
阿拉宁波 ālā níngbō
With its disyllabic form and no resemblance to pronouns in Mandarin, the first-person pronoun 阿拉 is quite distinctively Wu.

Figure 18.14 **Old mother's brother**
舅jiù | uncle 老娘舅 lǎo niángjiù
米饭要讲究 mǐfàn yào jiǎngjiū | be particular about rice
就吃老娘舅 jiù chī lǎo niángjiù | then eat at mother's brother's
老娘舅 is a regional chain restaurant known for its tasty rice (note the rice bowl icon). The Mandarin counterpart to 娘舅 is 舅舅. Note the repetition of the syllable jiù (究，就，舅), which no doubt is deliberate.

Figure 18.15 **Nanxiang dumpling shop**
南翔馒头店 nánxiáng mántóu diàn
This is one of the best-known traditional restaurants in Shanghai. To a northerner, 馒头 is plain steam bread; but in Shanghai, it is filled with meat inside.

Min/Taiwanese

The southern Min dialect and that in Taiwan are closely related. Not being mutually intelligible with other Chinese dialects, they retain many old phonetic and lexical features.

Figure 18.16 **Old early taste Taiwan beautiful food**
古早味台湾美食 gǔzǎo wèi táiwān měishí
中式料理 zhōngshì liàolǐ | Chinese style cooking
古早味 is a Min dialect word. 料理 is however Japanese in origin. This is seen in Vancouver's Chinatown.

Figure 18.17 **Grandma roast corn**

阿嬷の烧番卖 āmà no shāo fānmài

阿嬷 is grandma in the Min dialect. 烧番卖, also written as 烧番麦, is roasted corn on the cob. 番 is commonly used for things foreign, such as 番茄 'tomato'. Note the use of the Japanese particle の, instead of Chinese 的.

Figure 18.18 **Lake view restaurant**

湖景餐厅 hújǐng cāntīng

俗搁大碗 súgē dàwǎn | popular put big bowl

冷气开放 lěngqì kāifàng | cold air open release

俗搁大碗 is Min for 'cheap and good'. 冷气 'AC' would be 空调 in mainland China. This is near Sun Moon Lake in Taiwan.

Figure 18.19 **House in little family village**

厝内小眷村 cuònèi xiǎo juàncūn

This is a chain selling Taiwanese style milk tea. 厝 is a Min word and 眷村 are residential compounds built for Nationalist soldiers and their families when they first arrived in Taiwan. With people from all over China, 眷村 life developed its own characteristics including its foods.

Figure 18.20 **Each piece 4 yuan**

每粒4元 měi lì 4 yuán

水饺 shuǐjiǎo | water (boiled) dumpling

方记 fāng jì | Fang's

The measure word 粒, usually used for small objects like sesame seeds or medicine pills, is used more generally in Min, including for watermelons!

Mandarin

It needs to be noted that Mandarin is not a single dialect, but a family of dialects. Largely mutually intelligible, they can nonetheless differ in sound and vocabulary. Of the many Mandarin dialects, the Northeastern and the Southwestern varieties tend to be used more often for comic effect.

Figure 18.21 **Have matter no matter**
有事没事 yǒushì méishì (for no reason)
整点乐事 zhěngdiǎn lèshì | get some happy matter (Lay's)
整点 is distinctly Northeastern Mandarin. For some reason, this regional variety has been exploited extensively for comic effect.

Figure 18.22 **Spicy those year**
辣些年 làxiē nián
The name of this red chili shop uses a pun based on dialectal difference: 辣là is a mispronunciation of 那 nà and 那些年 means 'those years'. The inability to distinguish between 'n' and 'l' is a distinguishing feature of the chili loving speakers of southwest Mandarin.

Learning Outcomes

a. Gain greater awareness of dialectal differences.
b. Gain greater awareness of the relationship between Cantonese and classical Chinese.
c. Gain awareness of the use of the Rebus Principle in writing dialect words.

Suggested Learning Activities

1. If you can, take pictures of signs containing dialectal elements. Type them out and translate.
2. Using the dialectal words in this chapter, search online for more examples. Type them out and translate.

3. Using the online Cantonese dictionary CantoDict (cantonese.sheik.co .uk/dictionary/), look up the numbers 'one, three, six, ten'. Which consonants are not found in Mandarin?

4. Cite some examples of dialectal pronunciation, vocabulary, and grammar.

5. Cite some examples of Cantonese sharing similarities with classical Chinese.

6. If you are a speaker of a Chinese dialect, can you give examples of words that are unique to your dialect?

7. For dialect words that have no Mandarin counterparts, what characters tend to be chosen to write them?

19 The Chinese Diaspora

Chinese can be found in most parts of the world. The signs in this chapter are mainly from the United States. A few are from Kyrgyzstan.

Figure 19.1 **Flushing, New York**
But for the few English words that give away the location, Flushing in Queens New York city could well be mistaken for Taipei or Hong Kong.

Signs in the diaspora contexts are distinguished by the need to negotiate between Chinese and the local language(s), as Chinese is used to represent local contexts. Both meaning-based translation and sound-based transliteration are used, as well as a combination of the two. Also notable are the dialectal elements (for more examples of dialectal elements in signs, see Chapter 18). The language of the Chinese diaspora in North America is heavily Cantonese, as the earliest immigrants were from Cantonese-speaking areas of China. Cantonese has also been adopted as sort of a lingua franca. For example, in San Francisco's Chinatown, standard Cantonese as spoken in Guangzhou and Hong Kong is extensively used, especially with outsiders, even though the dominant dialect was Toishan, a sub-dialect of the Cantonese dialect family. Mandarin is increasingly common in the newer immigrant communities, for example in Los Angeles. Traditional characters are used as a rule, reflecting the dominance of traditional culture. The traditional vertical and right-to-left text orientation coexists with that of the modern horizontal and left-to-right format.

As seen in Boston's Chinatown, there are also cases of 'diaspora in diaspora' in the sense that some of the diaspora Chinese, such as Vietnamese Chinese, had already been away from China before coming to America.

Landmarks

Many Chinatowns are marked by traditional archways like this one seen in Boston and Portland, Oregon.

Figure 19.2 **Boston's Chinatown**
天下为公 tiānxià wèigōng
whole world for public good
The lines on the archway should both be read from right to left.

Figure 19.3 **Boston's Chinatown**
礼义廉耻 lǐ yì lián chǐ
courtesy, justice, integrity, sense of shame
This is the other side of the same archway

Figure 19.4 **Portland's Chinatown**
砵崙华埠 bōlún huábù
The discrepancy between the transliteration bólún and Portland can be explained by the Cantonese origin of the transliteration.

Figure 19.5 **Four seas one family**
四海一家 sìhǎi yìjiā
The phrase expresses the utopian desire for universal brotherhood.

Streets

Figure 19.6 **Elizabeth Street**
伊丽莎白街 yīlìshābái jiē
陈宇晖路 chén yǔhuī lù | Danny Chen Way
This is seen in New York's Chinatown. Elizabeth is transliterated by sound; 'street' is translated by meaning as 街. The sign below is in memory of Danny Chen, a Chinese American soldier who died in Afghanistan. The Chinese version is simply his name 陈宇晖 (in traditional characters) and 'way' is translated by meaning as 路 'road' (photo credit: Eric Cheng).

Figure 19.7 **Everett Street**
西北 xīběi | west north   爱和烈街 àihéliè jiē | Everett Street
This is in Portland's Chinatown. While àihéliè sounds quite different from Everett, its Cantonese pronunciation sounds closer.

Figure 19.8 **South King Street**
南景街 nánjǐng jiē | south scenery street
南第六大道 nán dìliù dàdào | south 6th Ave
This is in Seattle's Chinatown. Everything is translated by meaning, except King, which is transliterated as 景 which means 'scenery'. While 景 jǐng sounds quite different from king, its Cantonese pronunciation sounds quite close.

Figure 19.9 **Beach Street**
必珠街bìzhū jiē
This is in Boston's Chinatown. It is quite an unexpected rendition!

Businesses

Figure 19.10 **Boston Chinatown chamber of commerce welcomes you**
波士顿华埠商会欢迎您
bōshìdùn huábù shānghuì huānyíng nín

Figure 19.11 **Taste Chinatown food**
品尝华埠美食 pǐncháng huábù měishí
支持华埠商户 zhīchí huábù shānghù
support Chinatown businesses
特价泊车 tèjià bóchē | special price parking

Figure 19.12 **Waiwai**
威威 wēiwēi
姜葱白切鸡 jiāngcōng báiqiē jī
ginger scallion plain cut chicken
This is in Boston's Chinatown. Note how 威威 is
pronounced in Cantonese. Also note the so-called chop
suey font that Waiwai is written in.

Figure 19.13 **Gold fortune**
金财 jīn cái
Amazingly, Chinese, French, and English are all used, in addition to Vietnamese!

.14 **Great Wall winery**
hángchéng | great wall 酒庄 jiǔzhuāng | winery
ie Vietnamese transliteration Truong Thanh for the Great Wall.

9.15 **Chinese herbs**
参茸药材 nánběi háng sēnróng yàocái
north firm ginseng antler herbal medicine
Bac Hong' contains both Cantonese 'm' and Vietnamese 'c' (for k).

Figure 19.16 **Cantonese Sichuan food**
华记huá jì | Hua's 蜀餸shǔ sòng | Sichuan food
Both 'Wa' in 'Captain Wa' and 餸are Cantonese. But why is the food 蜀, the alias
for Sichuan? Only possible in the Chinese diaspora! This restaurant is in fact in
the heavily Chinese area of Richmond, Vancouver.

Alternative Romanization Schemes

Figure 19.17 **Great harmony restaurant**
大同饭店 dàtóng fàndiàn
This restaurant is in Seattle's Chinatown. The
discrepancy between Tai Tung and the Mandarin
Datong is explainable in terms of dialect and
alternative romanization, as大同is indeed
pronounced like Tai Tung in Cantonese and the
letter T in Tai is due to the alternative romanization.
饭店 is not the most common term for restaurant
and it can also mean hotel (photo credit Xu
Dongdong).

Figure 19.18 **Fresh Chinese kale**
新鲜芥兰 xīnxiān jièlán
The English translation surely looks unusual. Why is there 'R' in LARN? It is in
fact 国语罗马字, an older romanization system using letters to spell tones.
R marks the rising (2nd) tone. This is seen in Auckland, New Zealand.

Kyrgyzstan

A little-known fact is that there are Chinese-speaking Muslims in Central Asia called Dungans, scattered mostly along the Chui River dividing Kyrgyzstan and Kazakhstan. Their ancestors left Northwest China about 150 years ago after the failed Muslim uprising. A distinct characteristic of the Dungans is their use of alphabetic writing, including Arabic, Roman, and the current Cyrillic script.

Figure 19.19 **Muslim Chinese**
Хуэймин (回民)huímín | return people
This is a bilingual newspaper published by the Dungan Association of Kyrgyzstan. It is in both Dungan and Russian, using the Cyrillic script.

Figure 19.20 **Lucky restaurant**
йУнчи (运气)|yùnqì | luck
This restaurant is in Alexandrovka, the largest Dungan village 20 km west of the capital Bishkek. The Russian and Kyrgyz words, given above and below, mean 'café'.

Figure 19.21 **Hotpot**
Xoro (火锅) huǒguō | fire wok
This restaurant is in the Dungan village of Alexandrovka.

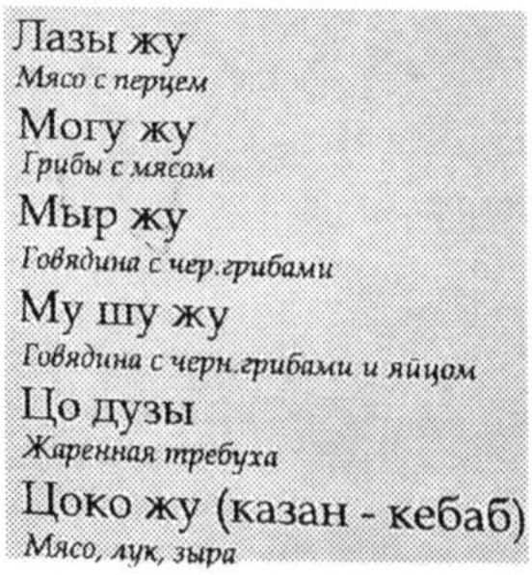

Лазы жу
Мясо с перцем
Могу жу
Грибы с мясом
Мыр жу
Говядина с чер.грибами
Му шу жу
Говядина с черн.грибами и яйцом
Цо дузы
Жаренная требуха
Цоко жу (казан - кебаб)
Мясо, лук, зыра

Figure 19.22 **Dungan dishes**
Лазы жу (辣子肉) làzǐ ròu | chili meat
Могу жу (蘑菇肉) mógū ròu | mushroom meat
Мыр жу (木耳肉) mù'ěr ròu | fungus meat
Му шу жу (木须肉) mù xū ròu | mooshoo meat
Цо дузы (炒肚子) chǎo dǔzi | fried tripe
Цоко жу (炒烤肉) chǎo kǎoròu | fried BBQ meat
This is part of a menu of a restaurant in Tokmok city. The lines under Dungan in smaller font are Russian translations.

Immigration Law and Accountants' Offices

All three offices below are in Alhambra Los Angeles, which has one of the largest Chinese populations in the United States.

Figure 19.23 **Same boat immigration**
同舟移民 tóngzhōu yímín | same boat move people

Figure 19.24 **American immigration office**
驻美移民事务所 zhùměi yímín shìwùsuǒ
station US move people affairs office
(American immigration agency)

Figure 19.25 **CPA**
智达会计 zhìdá kuàijì | wisdom achieve accounting

Associations

Many clannish and regional associations exist for diaspora Chinese. Earlier immigrants depend on them for support. Being older in style, the text orientation tends to go from right to left and the text is mostly in traditional characters. Sometimes, the English spelling reflects the dialectal origin.

The following associations are seen in the Chinatowns of Boston and Portland, Oregon.

Boston

Figure 19.26 **Senior association**
中华耆英会 zhōnghuá qíyīng huì
Chinese Senior Citizens Association

Figure 19.27 **Vietnam Cambodia Laos Chinese Association**
麻省越棉寮华人协会 máshěng yuèmiánliáo huárén xiéhuì
Massachusetts Vietnam Cambodia Laos Chinese Association
These Chinese had already been in Southeast Asia before coming to the United States.

Figure 19.28 **Huang clan family association**
黄氏宗亲会 huángshì zōngqīn huì
Note the name of the clan is Wong in Cantonese (Huang in Mandarin).

Portland, Oregon

Figure 19.29 **Chinese Association**
中华会馆 zhōnghuá huìguǎn
Chinese gathering place

Figure 19.30 **Hip Sing association**
协胜公会 xiéshèng gōnghuì
assist victory association
Note the difference in pronunciation between
Cantonese Hip Sing and Mandarin xiéshèng.

Figure 19.31 **Family and friend association**
至孝笃亲公所 zhìxiào dǔqīn gōngsuǒ
utmost filial devote family association
至诚孝友 zhìchéng xiàoyǒu
utmost sincere and filial to friends
笃爱亲仁 dǔ'ài qīnrén
love family and friends
The traditional format is like that of a
spring couplet.

Political Ads

Being two of the earliest regions of settlement for Chinese immigrants,
San Francisco and Boston have a significant Chinese population. Even
non-Chinese politicians are using Chinese-language campaign ads to
attract votes.

San Francisco

Figure 19.32 **Leno for mayor**
重整市府 chóngzhěng shìfǔ | re-organize city hall
迈步向前 màibù xiàngqián | march forward
里诺 lǐnuò | Leno
三藩市市长 sānfān shì shìzhǎng
San Francisco city mayor

Figure 19.33 **Vote for Martin Rawlings-Fein**
在选举旧金山教育委员会一席
zài xuǎnjǔ jiùjīnshān jiàoyù wěiyuánhuì yìxí
In electing SF's education board one seat
请投马文龙一票 qǐng tóu mǎ wénlóng yípiào
please cast Ma Wenlong a vote
The candidate's Chinese name notwithstanding, 马文龙 (Martin Rawlings-Fein)
is not Chinese.

Boston

Figure 19.34 **Healey & Driscoll**
希利&德里斯科 xīlì & délǐsīkē
为麻州的未来wèi mázhōu de wèilái | for Massachusetts state's future

Figure 19.35 **Fair pay tax**
公平缴税 gōngpíng jiǎoshuì

Learning Outcomes

a. Gain greater awareness of the diversity in writing format.
b. Gain familiarity with the translation strategies used in bilingual signs.
c. Gain greater appreciation for the role of Cantonese in the Chinese diaspora.

Suggested Learning Activities

1. If you are close to a Chinatown, take pictures of signs in Chinese. Type them out and translate.
2. Using 中国城 and 唐人街, search online for landmarks, street signs, and names of Chinese businesses. You can target a specific location by adding locations such as 纽约 'New York', 旧金山 'San Francisco', 洛杉矶 'Los Angeles', 伦敦 'London', and 悉尼 'Sydney'. You can also use traditional characters to bring up more examples. Type out the text in the signs and translate into English if it is not given.
3. Do you notice any differences due to the locale? Comment on them.
4. Identify translation strategies and possible mistakes in bilingual or multi-lingual signs.
5. If you are ethnic Chinese growing up outside of China, is the English spelling of your name different from that in pinyin? Why is this the case?

20 Foreign Infusion

In mainland China, Reform and Opening up in the last few decades has opened a floodgate of foreign infusion. Foreign businesses such as KFC, Starbucks, Walmart, McDonalds, and Carrefour are seen everywhere. The ones given in this chapter are by no means complete. For example, the British supermarket chain 乐购 (Tesco) and German 麦德龙 (Metro) are not given here.

There have also been many loanwords. Some of the loanwords have become so much a part of the Chinese lexicon that their foreign origin may not even be clear to all. The word for cookie 曲奇, an English loanword by way of Cantonese, is a particularly good example.

Apart from the social and cultural implications, the influx of things foreign presents quite a challenge to Chinese with its non-phonetic script. Various accommodation strategies have been used to represent foreign words with Chinese characters, including meaning translation, phonetic transliteration, or a combination of both, resulting in varying degrees of semantic and phonetic approximation. Incidentally, the fact that the Rebus (phonetic loan) Principle is extensively used for phonetic transliterations, whereby Chinese characters are used only for their sounds without regard to their meanings, show that the persistent ideographic myth concerning Chinese characters is untrue.

Since some of these foreign brands were first introduced into mainland China through dialect speaking areas such as the Cantonese-speaking Hong Kong, phonetic transliterations quite often do not sound very close the original foreign words in Mandarin Chinese. For more information about dialects, especially Cantonese, see Chapters 18 and 19.

Along with real foreign names, there are also some 'pseudo-foreign' ones. While this may reflect obsession with things foreign, there may also be functional reasons. One possibility is to overcome the inherent limitation in the choice of names. Chinese names are short while foreign ones can be much longer, which allows more combinatorial possibilities. Using foreign sounding syllables, which do not need to have transparent meanings, also obviates the almost obligatory need to choose auspicious characters.

Fast-food Restaurant

Figure 20.1 **Kentucky**
肯德基 kěndéjī
KFC ranks first in the number of stores and the earliest entry into the Chinese market. Note that the Chinese transliteration is only for the K of KFC.

Figure 20.2 **McDonald's**
麦当劳 màidāngláo
Why is 麦当劳 used for McDonald's when it doesn't even sound close? The fact is that it came via Cantonese, which sounds much closer to English, down to the 'Mc' part (麦 is pronounced mak). The tonal pattern 'low high low' fits the stress pattern of McDonald quite nicely too. McDonald's had entered Hong Kong earlier in 1975.

Figure 20.3 **Pizza Hut**
必胜客欢乐餐厅 bìshèngkè huānlè cāntīng
must win guest happy diner
The semi-transliteration 必胜客 also means: must win guest.

Figure 20.4 **Subway**
赛百味 sài bǎiwèi | exceed 100 flavor
This transliteration also has meaning. In Taiwan it is literally called a sub-marine burger: 潜艇堡 qiántǐng bǎo.

Figure 20.5 **Domino's pizza**
达美乐比萨 dáměilè bǐsà | reach beauty happy pizza
While the whole name is based on transliteration, the first part 达美乐 tries to
use nice-sounding characters, but 比萨 is pure transliteration.

Figure 20.6 **Starbucks**
想喝星巴克 xiǎng hē xīngbākè | would like to drink Starbucks
没时间排队 méi shíjiān páiduì | no time to line up
The Chinese name is a combination of meaning translation (星=star) and
transliteration (巴克=buck).

Figure 20.7 **Burger King**
汉堡王 hànbǎo wáng | hamburger king
This is a mixture of transliteration (汉堡=Hamburger) and meaning
translation (王=king).

Figure 20.8 **Papa John's**
棒约翰 bàng yuēhàn | awesome John
Note the Chinese name of this American pizza chain deviates in meaning from
the original name.

Figure 20.9 **Carl's Jr.**
卡乐星 kǎlè xīng | Carl star
Although there is a star in the logo, it is not in the English name. The Chinese name does include it.

Chain Stores

Figure 20.10 **Walmart**
沃尔玛 wò'ěrmǎ
This is pure transliteration, without any attempt at choosing auspicious sounding characters.

Figure 20.11 **Carrefour**
家乐福 jiālèfú | home happy blessing
This is a French hypermarket chain.

Figure 20.12 **Best Buy**
百思买 bǎisīmǎi | 100 think buy
The meanings of the characters definitely do not mean 'best buy'!

Figure 20.13 **Watsons**
屈臣氏 qūchén shì
This transliteration is via Cantonese. But it also sounds like a possible
Chinese name.

A Few Food Items

Figure 20.14 **Caffe latte**
咖啡拿铁 kāfēi nátiě | coffee wield iron
美式咖啡 měishì kāfēi | American style coffee
杯bēi | cup
The characters 咖啡 both have a 口 component indicating its transliteration
status. The transliteration nature of 拿铁 is not as obvious. The original
meanings of the characters are rather scary: wield iron.

Figure 20.15 **Cookie**
杏花楼 xìnghuā lóu | apricot flower building
双色曲奇 shuāngsè qǔqí | double color cookie
two-tone cookies
品位粤式糕点 pǐnwèi yuèshì gāodiǎn
high class Cantonese style pastry
曲奇 is a recent loanword from English via
Cantonese, which pronounces it as kukkei. The
Mandarin pronunciation qǔqí is quite different
from English. As an instance of phonetic loan, the
original meanings of the two characters 'tune' and
'strange' are quite irrelevant. 杏花楼 is a
venerable Cantonese restaurant in Shanghai also
known for its line of food products.

免治牛肉粥（中）Minced Beef Congee

Figure 20.16 **Minced**

免治牛肉粥(中) miǎnzhì niúròu zhōu (zhōng)

minced beef congee (medium)

免治 is borrowed from English 'minced', possibly via Cantonese.

Figure 20.17 **Toast and sandwich**

厚片吐司 hòupiàn tǔsī | thick slice toast +饮品yǐnpǐn | beverage
（限30元以下饮品 xiàn 30 yuán yǐxià yǐnpǐn）
(limit to below 30 yuan beverage)

阳光三明治 yángguāng sānmíngzhì | sunny sandwich+饮品yǐnpǐn | beverage
（红茶、绿茶、奶茶 hóngchá lǜchá nǎichá | black tea, green tea, milk tea
吐司 and 三明治 are from English 'toast' and 'sandwich' respectively.

Figure 20.18 **Ciabatta/bagel**

巧巴达/贝果 qiǎobādá/bèiguǒ | ciabatta/bagel + 饮品 yǐnpǐn | beverage
（限30元以下饮品 xiàn 30 yuán yǐxià yǐnpǐn）
(limit to below 30 yuan beverage)

Figure 20.19 **Morton salt**

莫顿牌精制盐 mòdùn pái jīngzhì yán

Morton brand fine manufacture salt

未加碘 wèi jiā diǎn | not add iodine

源自于美国的百年品牌

yuánzì yú měiguó de bǎinián pǐnpái

source from in US 100 year brand

净含量：737克 jìng hánliàng:737 kè

net content: 737 gram

It is surprising that such a basic item is imported.
未, 自, and 于 are classical Chinese for 没有, 从,
and 在 respectively.

Japanese

Japanese businesses are also very common in China.

Figure 20.20 **Number 1 house**
壹番屋 yìfān wū | Ichibanya
This is a Japanese-style restaurant also written as 壹番屋, featuring curry dishes.

Figure 20.21 **Shabu-shabu**
呷哺呷哺 xiāfǔxiāfǔ
Shabu-shabu comes from Japanese meaning 'hotpot'.

Figure 20.22 **Teppanyaki**
铁板 tiěbǎn | iron plate
达人 dárén | master
铁板 is from 铁板烧 Teppanyaki.

Figure 20.23 **Izakaya**
日式居酒屋 rìshì jūjiǔwū
Japan style stay drink house
居酒屋 is from Japanese 'izakaya'.

Figure 20.24 **Whole family**
全家 quánjiā
This is a Japanese convenience-store chain seen all over Shanghai. Its Japanese pronunciation is the transliteration of Family Mart: ファミリーマート.

Figure 20.25 **Lawson**
罗森 luósēn 便利店biànlì diàn | convenience store
Despite its Anglo sounding name, it is a Japanese company, albeit originally
started in the United States.

Figure 20.26 **Bento**
六星便当 liù xīng biàndāng | six-star bento (box lunch)
便当 is a loanword from Japanese. It is used more often in Taiwan than in China.

Figure 20.27 **Set meal**
排骨定食 páigǔ dìngshí | rib set meal
香鱼定食 xiāngyú dìngshí | ayu set meal
鲭鱼定食 qīngyú dìngshí | salmon set meal
定食 is from Japanese *teishoku* 'set meal', comprising of rice, soup, and a side dish.

Figure 20.28 **Story**
暖冬物语 nuǎndōng wùyǔ
warm winter story
物语 is 'story' in Japanese.

Korean

Figure 20.29 **Korean food**
韩国食品 hánguó shípǐn
This is seen in Shanghai.

.30 **Korean BBQ shop**
ōnghè | pine crane 韩国烧烤店 hánguó shāokǎo diàn
ie similarity and difference in pronunciation for crane between Korean 'hak' and Mandarin 'he'. 'Hak' is
borrowed from Chinese and retains the older pronunciation. This is in San Diego, United States.

Sinicization of Foreign Elements

An interesting phenomenon is the Sinicization of foreign elements after they enter Chinese. They come to be used as if they are native Chinese words. One such example is the use of 嗨 hāi 'high' as a verb, as can be seen in the examples below. It can even be followed by a resultative complement: 嗨翻 fān 'get high to the point of being head over heels'; it can also be used as a resultative complement itself: 玩嗨 'have fun to the point of being high'.

Figure 20.31 **High together**
一起嗨 yìqǐ hāi | together high 海底捞 hǎidǐ lāo | sea-bottom scoop
This is a popular hotpot restaurant. The 嗨 comes from English 'high' but has become a verb meaning 'be high spirited'. Not only does 嗨 sound like 'high', it also resembles the character 海.

Figure 20.32 **High upside down Monday**
麦当劳 màidāngláo | McDonald's
嗨翻星期一 hāifān xīngqī yī | high upside down Monday
嗨 is followed by the resultative complement 翻 'upside down'. The nativized 嗨 can even be used as a resultative complement itself such as 玩嗨 'have fun till high'.

Figure 20.33 **Most in**
最zuì | most
Although we can say 'the in crowd' in English, 'most in' seems to be quite new!

Pseudo-Foreign

There are also pseudo-foreign-sounding brands such as '波司登 (bosi-deng)' (see 20.38). Also seen is the mixing of scripts with direct inclusion of foreign elements, such as AA 制 'each paying for own share' known to all in China but opaque to people outside. The profusion of (often gratuitous) foreign elements is a phenomenon worthy of serious study.

Figure 20.34 **Home delivery**
自助点餐 zìzhù diǎncān | self-order and 宅急送zháijísòng | home deliver
点餐不排队 diǎncān bù páiduì | order no lineup
随时随地享美味 suíshí suídì xiǎng měiwèi | anytime anywhere enjoy good foods
宅急送 is a Chinese company modeled on the Japanese 宅急便. This is used by KFC to promote their home delivery service.

Figure 20.35 **Japanese fine image**
和良形象 héliáng xíngxiàng
This Japanese-sounding name of a hair salon in
Shanghai seems to be partly Chinese. Its owners
are from Tokyo, Shanghai, and Seoul.

Figure 20.36 **Youngor**
雅戈尔 yǎgē'ěr
This is a textile clothing company, headquartered in
Ningbo Zhejiang province. While following the
transliteration practice of using characters mostly for
their sounds, the character 雅 does mean 'elegant'.

Figure 20.37 **Chlitina**
克丽缇娜 kèlìtínà
This skin-care and beauty salon is founded in Taiwan. It is hard to tell what
language Chlitina is based on, with its unusual consonant cluster at
the beginning.

Figure 20.38 **Bosideng**
波司登 bōsīdēng
This pseudo-foreign sounding brand seems to pop up everywhere, on trains
and airplanes. It is a major purveyor of down products headquartered in
Changshu, Jiangsu province. It was ostensibly coined to sound like Boston,
which is otherwise transliterated as 波士顿 bōshìdùn.

Figure 20.39 **Wedome**
味多美 wèiduōměi | taste much beautiful
It is a bakery based in Beijing. It is not clear how the spelling comes about.

Learning Outcomes

a. Know the difference between meaning translation and phonetic transliteration.
b. Gain awareness of the dialectal origin of some phonetic transliterations.
c. Gain greater sensitivity to the issue of character choice in phonetic transliteration.

Suggested Learning Activities

1. Search online for examples of foreign businesses translated into Chinese. Is phonetic transliteration or meaning translation (or a combination) used?
2. Are there alternative translations?
3. How are the characters chosen?
4. If there is a discrepancy between the Chinese rendition and the pronunciation of the foreign words, offer an explanation as to why that is the case.
5. Using Google Translate or other translation apps, translate some English signs into Chinese and judge the quality of the translations.
6. Translate signs from English to Chinese and decide whether phonetic transliteration or meaning translation (or a combination) is used.
7. Find examples of foreign words being integrated into Chinese grammar.
8. Find out if there are other pseudo-foreign names of Chinese businesses.

21 (Supplemental): Mistranslated Signs

Many signs in urban areas are bilingual in Chinese and English. It cannot escape the notice of even the most casual bilingual observer that many such signs are woefully (and sometimes hilariously) mistranslated.

Mistakes can result from wrong segmentation, wrong word choice, wrong grammar, or inappropriate style, which is particularly important in Chinese. Mistakes can also result from missing crucial information or lack of understanding of English. There are also the 'innovative analogies', which give rise to non-existent English words. Also frequently observed are inconsistencies, wavering between the two strategies of pinyin transliteration and meaning translation.

The inclusion of mistranslated signs can be pedagogically useful in more than one way (Shang and Xie 2020). Studying mistranslated signs is an exercise in contrastive analysis. Through detailed analysis of the causes of the mistakes, such signs can be used as negative examples in the teaching of both Chinese and English. They can also be useful to the study and practice of translation.

Wrong Segmentation

The Chinese writing convention is not to leave space between words. This presents a challenge to both readers and computers in segmentation, that is, grouping unbroken strings of characters into words or phrases. Mistakes in translation often result due to the wrong segmentation, especially when the translation is done by computers.

Figure 21.1 **Early restaurant**
早餐厅 zǎocān tīng | early meal hall (breakfast hall)
What is 'early restaurant'? The mistake results from the wrong segmentation. The middle character 餐 can be grouped with the last character to mean 'restaurant' as well as with the first character to mean 'breakfast'.

Figure 21.2 **Carefully slide**
小心地滑 xiǎoxīn dìhuá | small heart ground slippery
(careful, ground is slippery)
This mistake results from grouping 地 with the adjective 小心 to mean
'carefully'; 地 is used as an adverbial marker instead of 'ground'.

Figure 21.3 **Day and convenience store**
天和便利店 tiānhé biànlì diàn | Tianhe convenience store
The English seems too outlandish to be believable, but this was actually seen in
Lijiang Yunnan. The second character 和 is part of the name天和, but the
translation software construed it as 'and', the most frequent meaning of 和. The
owner of the store wasn't entirely convinced when the error was pointed out to
him, as he had paid good money for the translation.

Missing Spacing between English Words

The Chinese convention of not having a space between words has
somehow been transferred to English. But the phenomenon is more
common than expected.

Figure 21.4 **Xinjianginternatioalbigbazaar**
新疆国际大巴扎 xīnjiāng guójì dà bāzhā
Xinjiang international big bazaar
宴艺大剧院 yàn yì dà jùyuàn | banquet art big theater
The translation is not problematic, but no spaces were provided between the
English words!

Incomplete Translation

Some mistranslations are incomplete.

Figure 21.5 **Careful soup**
小心汤烫 xiǎoxīn tāng tàng | small heart soup hot
(Careful. Soup is hot.)
The crucial part about the soup being hot is missing.

Figure 21.6 **Shared bicycle access**
共享单车禁止入内 gòngxiǎng dānchē jìnzhǐ rùnèi
shared bike forbid enter
Missing 'forbid', the sign has the opposite meaning.

Incomprehension

Some mistranslations seem to be due to insufficient command of English.

Figure 21.7 **Glass care**
小心玻璃 xiǎoxīn bōli | small heart glass (Careful! Glass is fragile)
'glass care' in English means 'to take care of glass', which is entirely different from the meaning in Chinese 'being careful about the possible breaking of glass'.

Figure 21.8 **Mainly preserved architecture**
大连市重点保护建筑 dàlián shì zhòngdiǎn bǎohù jiànzhù
Dalian city key protect architecture
中国银行旧址 zhōngguó yínháng jiùzhǐ | China bank old site
大连市人民政府 dàlián shì rénmín zhèngfǔ
Dalian city people government
In addition to the wrong translation for 保护, 重点 is also mistranslated. That it was an official plaque put up by the city government is quite embarrassing.

Wrong Sense

Many characters or word forms in Chinese have more than one meaning. Choosing the wrong sense, most likely done by the computer, can lead to nonsensical or hilarious results.

Figure 21.9 **Beware of to meet**
当心碰头 dāngxīn pèngtóu | careful hit head
(Careful with bumping the head.)
In addition to bumping the head, 碰头 can also have the metaphorical meaning 'to meet'.

Figure 21.10 **Exports slide**
滑道出口 huádào chūkǒu | slide path out opening (slide exit)
Unlike 入口, which can only mean 'entrance' and not 'import', 出口 can mean both 'exit' and 'export'.

Analogy Running Amok

There are mistranslations that don't seem to be attributable to anything but sheer creative analogy.

Figure 21.11 **Fresh your life**
新鲜你的生活 xīnxiān nǐ de shēnghuó
This was seen in a store in Shanghai. Does it mean 'freshen your life'? Note the Chinese, on which the translation is based, is also ungrammatical.

Figure 21.12 **Heartness, loveness**
用心 yòngxīn | use heart (attentive)
关爱 guān'ài | concern love
愉悦 yúyuè | happy pleasure
Where do 'heartness' and 'loveness' come from?

Inconsistency in Road Signs

Shang (2020) observed that there is much 'wrestling' regarding language choice when signed are designed. Similarly, there are two competing strategies when rendering Chinese road signs into English: meaning translation and phonetic transliteration. To English speakers, meaning translation is easier for comprehension but not good for asking directions from Chinese people; the phonetic transliteration option is the opposite: opaque in meaning but easier for asking directions. Ideally, both phonetic transliterations and meaning translations should be given, as both are important for foreign visitors, for whom the English is intended after all. Unfortunately, only the phonetic transliteration option was adopted for Beijing's subway signs ahead of the 2022 Winter Olympics.

There seems to be little consistency in rendering street names into English, as can be seen in Figures 21.13–21.17. Inconsistency naturally leads to confusion.

Figure 21.13 **Jinshan middle road**
堇山中路 jīnshān zhōng lù | Jin mount mid road

Figure 21.14 **Middle Yanggao road**
杨高中路 yánggāo zhōng lù | Yanggao mid road

Figure 21.15 **Jinshan zhonglu**
堇山中路 jīnshān zhōng lù | Jin mount mid road
All three signs above contain中, with the meaning of 'middle'. But they are different in how 中路 is rendered. The top one translates it into 'middle' and puts it before the word road; the second one puts it at the beginning. The top one follows the Chinese word order, but the second one is more idiomatic English. The last sign simply gives the pinyin 'zhong', which is quite opaque in meaning but perhaps more helpful to foreigners asking directions.

Figure 21.16 **South Qilianshan Road**
祁连山南路 qíliánshān nán lù | Qilianshan south road

Figure 21.17 **Nanyangjin Road**
南洋泾路 nán yángjīng lù | south yangjing road
Both signs above are found in Shanghai's subway. They both contain 南 'south'.
The first sign uses meaning translation (also the more idiomatic word order for
English), but the second one uses phonetic transliteration instead. One more
difference: the 南 is placed before road in the first one but at the beginning in
the second.

Stylistic Infelicity

As the style of public signs is quite specific, any deviation from the
conventionally accepted style will appear strange.

Figure 21.18 **Please have no no spiked shoes**
请勿穿钉鞋 qǐngwù chuān dīngxié
please don't wear nailed shoes
This was seen on the grounds of Confucius' Mansion in his hometown Qufu.
The Chinese is stylistically appropriate with the standard 请勿. But the English
translation sounds like baby talk.

Figure 21.19 **Women**
妇人 fùrén | woman person
The Chinese translation is stylistically quite inappropriate, being quite
old fashioned.

Carelessness

Typos are a common occurrence in bilingual signs.

Figure 21.20 **No pest allowed**
禁带宠物入内 jìn dài chǒngwù rùnèi
forbid bring pets enter in
Was it wrong choice of word or was it the careless reversal of letters (pets>pest)?
Pet owners will not be pleased!

Learning Outcomes

a. Gain greater sensitivity to mistakes in translation.
b. Be able to analyze the reasons for mistranslations.

Suggested Learning Activities

1. Search online for Chinese signs with bad English translations. The website https://english.com/ has mistranslated signs from many languages.
2. Analyze the mistakes and identify the type of mistranslations.
3. Correct the translations.
4. Select some road signs in Chinese and translate them into English. Discuss available choices between meaning translation and phonetic translation and the pros and cons of each.
5. Using Google Translate or other translation apps, translate Chinese signs (including the mistranslated ones in this chapter) into English and judge the quality of the translations.

REFERENCES

Guo, G and Li, B (2017). Linguistic Landscape of China: A Case Study of the Language Use of Shop Signs in Wuhan. *Studies in Literature and Language*, 15(1): 1–9. doi:10.3968/9816

Kubler, C (1993). *Read Chinese Signs* [with Hsiaojung Sharon L. Chi]. Boston: Cheng & Tsui Company.

Li, C and Thompson, S (1981). *Mandarin Chinese. A Functional Reference Grammar*. Berkeley, California: University of California Press.

Shang, G (2020). Wrestling between English and Pinyin Language Politics and Ideologies of Coding Street Names in China. *Journal of Language and Politics*, 19(4): 624–625. doi.org/10.1075/jlp.19072.sha

Shang, G and Xie, F (2020). Is "Poor" English in Linguistic Landscape Useful for EFL Teaching and Learning? Perspectives of EFL Teachers in China. *International Journal of Applied Linguistics*, 30(1): 35–49.

Wang, J (2013). Linguistic Landscape of China – A Case Study of Shop Signs in Beijing. *Studies in Literature & Language*, 6(1): 40–47.

Zhang, ZS (2016). A Multi-dimensional Corpus Study of Mixed Compounds in Chinese. (2016). In Hongyin Tao Ed. *Integrating Chinese Linguistic Research and Language Teaching and Learning*. Amsterdam: John Benjamins. 215–238.

Zhang, ZS (2017). *Dimensions of Variation in Written Chinese*. Abingdon: Routledge.

INDEX OF FIGURES

(cont.)

(*cont.*)

(cont.)

(*cont.*)

(cont.)

(cont.)

(*cont.*)

(*cont.*)

(*cont.*)

(cont.)

(*cont.*)

(cont.)

(*cont.*)

Index of Figures

(cont.)

Printed in the United States
by Baker & Taylor Publisher Services